CAMBRIDGE LIBRARY COLLECTION

Books of enduring scholarly value

Literary Studies

This series provides a high-quality selection of early printings of literary works, textual editions, anthologies and literary criticism which are of lasting scholarly interest. Ranging from Old English to Shakespeare to early twentieth-century work from around the world, these books offer a valuable resource for scholars in reception history, textual editing, and literary studies.

Milton

Ranking among the greatest of all English poets, John Milton (1608–74) was an influential thinker during a particularly volatile period in his nation's history. His supreme masterpiece *Paradise Lost* forms one of the pillars of English literature. The literary scholar and historian Sir Walter Alexander Raleigh (1861–1922) was educated at University College London and King's College, Cambridge. Following posts at Liverpool and Glasgow, he was appointed Professor of English Literature at Oxford University, where he also served as an adviser to the Clarendon Press. This work, first published in 1900, is based upon lectures he gave the previous year as Clark Lecturer in English Literature at Trinity College, Cambridge. Admired by the critic William Empson, it is a penetrating study of the great poet and contains a biographical sketch as well as lucid analyses of Milton's use of language and its significant influence.

Milton

WALTER ALEXANDER RALEIGH

CAMBRIDGE
UNIVERSITY PRESS

CAMBRIDGE UNIVERSITY PRESS

Cambridge, New York, Melbourne, Madrid, Cape Town,
Singapore, São Paolo, Delhi, Mexico City

Published in the United States of America by Cambridge University Press, New York

www.cambridge.org
Information on this title: www.cambridge.org/9781108057356

© in this compilation Cambridge University Press 2013

This edition first published 1900
This digitally printed version 2013

ISBN 978-1-108-05735-6 Paperback

MILTON

MILTON

BY

WALTER RALEIGH

Author of
'Style,' 'The English Novel,' &c.

LONDON
EDWARD ARNOLD
1900

TO

R. A. M. STEVENSON

WHOSE RADIANT AND SOARING INTELLIGENCE

ENLIGHTENED AND GUIDED ME

DURING THE YEARS OF OUR LOST COMPANIONSHIP

THIS UNAVAILING TRIBUTE OF

MEMORY AND LOVE

CONTENTS

INTRODUCTION

CHAPTER I

JOHN MILTON

CHAPTER II

THE PROSE WORKS

CHAPTER III

Paradise Lost : The Scheme

CHAPTER IV

Paradise Lost : The Actors. The Later Poems

CONTENTS

CHAPTER V

The Style of Milton : Metre and Diction

CHAPTER VI

The Style of Milton; and its Influence on English Poetry

EPILOGUE

INTRODUCTION

FRANCIS BACON, in one of his prose fragments, draws a memorable distinction between "arts mechanical" and "sciences of conceit." "In arts mechanical," he says, "the first device comes shortest, and time addeth and perfecteth. But in sciences of conceit the first author goeth farthest, and time leeseth and corrupteth. . . . In the former, many wits and industries contributed in one. In the latter, many men's wits spent to deprave the wit of one."

I fear that literary criticism of the kind that I propose to myself in these chapters on Milton must be classified with the "sciences of conceit." Indeed, Bacon puts it out of question that he himself would so have regarded it, for he goes on to explain how, after the deliverances of a master, "then begin men to aspire to the second prizes, to be a profound interpreter and commentor, to be a sharp champion and defender, to be a methodical compounder and abridger. And this is the

B

unfortunate succession of wits which the world hath yet had, whereby the patrimony of all knowledge goeth not on husbanded and improved, but wasted and decayed."

The blow is aimed at the scholastic philosophers, but it falls heavy on the critics of literature, on all who "aspire to the second prizes," or who think "that a borrowed light can increase the original light from whom it is taken." It is a searching arraignment of all who set themselves to expound in words the meaning and purpose of a master of verbal expression. Yet the very breadth of the indictment brings comfort and a means of escape. For the chief difficulties of an attempt to understand and judge Milton are difficulties inherent in the nature, not only of all criticism in the large sense, but also of all reading. In this association with great spirits which we call reading we receive but what we give, and take away only what we are fit to carry. Milton himself has stated the doctrine in its most absolute form, and has sought an enhanced authority for it by attributing it to the Christ—

Who reads
Incessantly, and to his reading brings not
A spirit and judgment equal or superior
(And what he brings what needs he elsewhere seek ?)
Uncertain and unsettled still remains,
Deep versed in books and shallow in himself,
Crude or intoxicate, collecting toys

And trifles for choice matters, worth a spunge,
As children gathering pebbles on the shore.

Literally taken, this is the negation of all the
higher functions of criticism, and the paralysis of
all learning. Only his peers, it is argued, can
read Shakespeare intelligently ; and, as if that did
not give him few enough readers, they are further
told that they will be wasting their time! But
love, unlike this proud Stoicism, is humble, and
contented with a little. I would put my apology
in the language of love rather than of philosophy.
I know that in Shakespeare, or in Milton, or in
any rare nature, as in Faire Virtue, the mistress of
Philarete—

There is some concealèd thing
So each gazet limiting,
He can see no more of merit
Than beseems his worth and spirit.

The appreciation of a great author asks knowledge and industry before it may be attempted,
but in the end it is the critic, not the author, who
is judged by it, and, where his sympathies have
been too narrow, or his sight too dim, condemned
without reprieve, and buried without a tombstone.

Imperfect sympathy, that eternal vice of criticism, is sometimes irremediable, sometimes caused
by imperfect knowledge. It takes forms as various
as the authors whom it misjudges. In the case of
Shakespeare, when we attempt to estimate him, to

gauge him, to see him from all sides, we become almost painfully conscious of his immensity. We can build no watch-tower high enough to give us a bird's-eye view of that " globe of miraculous continents." We are out of breath when we attempt to accompany him on his excursions, where he,

> through strait, rough, dense, or rare,
> With head, hands, wings, or feet pursues his way,
> And swims, or sinks, or wades, or creeps, or flies.

He moves so easily and so familiarly among human passions and human emotions, is so completely at home in all societies and all companies, that he makes us feel hide-bound, prejudiced and ill-bred, by the side of him. We have to widen our conception of human nature in order to think of him as a man. How hard a thing it is to conceive of Shakespeare as of a human spirit, embodied and conditioned, whose affections, though higher mounted than ours, yet, when they stooped, stooped with the like wing, is witnessed by all biographies of Shakespeare, and by many thousands of the volumes of criticism and commentary that have been written on his works. One writer is content to botanise with him—to study plant-lore, that is, with a theatrical manager, in his hard-earned leisure, for teacher. Another must needs read the Bible with him, although, when all is said, Shakespeare's study was but little on the Bible. Others elect to

keep him to music, astronomy, law, hunting, hawk-
ing, fishing. He is a good companion out of doors,
and some would fain keep him there, to make a
country gentleman of him. His incorrigible pre-
occupation with humanity, the ruling passion and
employment of his life, is beyond the range of their
complete sympathy ; they like to catch him out of
hours, to draw him aside and bespeak his interest,
for a few careless minutes, in the trades and pastimes that bulk so largely and so seriously in their
own perspective of life. They hardly know what
to make of his "unvalued book"; but they know
that he was a great man, and to have bought a
wool-fell or a quarter of mutton from him, that
would have been something! Only the poet-critics
attempt to see life, however brokenly, through
Shakespeare's eyes, to let their enjoyment keep
attendance upon his. And from their grasp, too,
he escapes by sheer excess.

In the case of Milton the imperfection of our
sympathy is due to other causes. In the first
place, we know him as we do not know Shakespeare. The history of his life can be, and has
been, minutely written. The affairs of his time,
political and religious, have been recorded with
enormous wealth of detail ; and this wealth, falling
into fit hands, has given us those learned modern
historians to whom the seventeenth century means
a period of five thousand two hundred and

eighteen weeks. Milton's own attitude towards these affairs is in no way obscure; he has explained it with great fulness and candour in numerous publications, so that it would be easy to draw up a declaration of his chief tenets in politics and religion. The slanders of his adversaries he met again and again with lofty passages of self-revelation. "With me it fares now," he remarks in one of these, "as with him whose outward garment hath been injured and ill-bedighted; for having no other shift, what help but to turn the inside outwards, especially if the lining be of the same, or, as it is sometimes, much better." In his poetry, too, he delights to reveal himself, to take the knowing reader into his confidence, to honour the fit audience with a confession.

But the difficulty is there none the less. Few critics have found Milton too wide or too large for them; many have found him too narrow, which is another form of imperfect sympathy. His lack of humour has alienated the interest of thousands. His ardent advocacy of toleration in the noblest of his prose treatises has been belittled by a generation which prides itself on that flaccid form of benevolence, and finds the mere repeal of the Licensing Act the smallest part of it. His pamphlets on divorce and on government have earned him the reputation of a theorist and

dreamer. The shrewd practical man finds it
easy to despise him. The genial tolerant man,
whose geniality of demeanour towards others is a
kind of quit-rent paid for his own moral laxity,
regards him as a Pharisee. The ready humourist
devises a pleasant and cheap entertainment by
dressing Adam and Eve in modern garments
and discussing their relations in the jargon of
modish frivolity. Even the personal history of
the poet has been made to contribute to the gaiety
of nations, and the flight of Mary Powell, the
first Mrs. Milton, from the house in Aldersgate
Street, has become something of a stock comic
episode in the history of English literature. So
heavy is the tax paid, even by a poet, for deficiency
in breadth and humour. Almost all men are less
humorous than Shakespeare ; but most men are
more humorous than Milton, and these, it is to
be feared, having suffered themselves to be
dragooned by the critics into professing a distant
admiration for *Paradise Lost*, have paid their last
and utmost tribute to the genius of its author.

It may be admitted without hesitation that his
lonely greatness rather forces admiration on us
than attracts us. That unrelenting intensity ;
that lucidity, as clear as air and as hard as agate ;
that passion which burns with a consuming heat
or with a blinding light in all his writings, have
endeared him to none. It is impossible to take

one's ease with Milton, to induce him to forget
his principles for a moment in the name of social
pleasure.   The most genial of his personal sonnets
is addressed to Henry Lawrence, the son of the
President of Cromwell's Council, and is an invita-
tion to dinner.   The repast promised is "light
and choice"; the guest is apostrophised, somewhat formidably, as "Lawrence, of virtuous father,
virtuous son," and is reminded, before he has
dined, that

> He who of these delights can judge, and spare
> To interpose them oft, is not unwise.

But the qualities that make Milton a poor
boon-companion are precisely those which combine to raise his style to an unexampled loftiness,
a dignity that bears itself easily in society greater
than human.   To attain to this height it was
needful that there should be no aimless expatiation
of the intellect, no facile diffusion of the sympathies over the wide field of human activity and
human character.   All the strength of mind and
heart and will that was in Milton went into the
process of raising himself.   He is like some giant
palm-tree; the foliage that sprang from it as it
grew has long since withered, the stem rises
gaunt and bare; but high up above, outlined
against the sky, is a crown of perennial verdure.

It is essential for the understanding of Milton

that we should take account of the rare simplicity
of his character. No subtleties ; no tricks of the
dramatic intellect, which dresses itself in a hundred
masquerading costumes and peeps out of a thousand spy-holes ; no development, one might almost
say, only training, and that self-imposed. There
is but one Milton, and he is throughout one
and the same, in his life, in his prose, and in his
verse ; from those early days, when we find him,
an uncouth swain,

> With eager thought warbling his Doric lay,

to the last days when, amid a swarm of disasters,
he approved himself like Samson, and earned for
himself the loftiest epitaph in the language, his
own—

> Nothing is here for tears, nothing to wail
> Or knock the breast ; no weakness, no contempt,
> Dispraise, or blame ; nothing but well and fair,
> And what may quiet us in a death so noble.

The world has not wholly misunderstood or
failed to appreciate this extraordinary character,
as one curious piece of evidence will serve to
show. Milton is one of the most egotistic of
poets. He makes no secret of the high value he
sets upon his gifts—" gifts of God's imparting,"
as he calls them, " which I boast not, but thank-
fully acknowledge, and fear also lest at my
certain account they be reckoned to me many

rather than few." Before he has so much as begun his great poem he covenants with his reader "that for some few years yet I may go on trust with him toward the payment of what I am now indebted, as being a work not to be raised from the heat of youth or the vapours of wine ; . . . nor to be obtained by the invocation of dame Memory and her siren daughters, but by devout prayer to that eternal Spirit, who can enrich with all utterance and knowledge, and sends out his seraphim, with the hallowed fire of his altar, to touch and purify the lips of whom he pleases ; to this must be added industrious and select reading, steady observation, insight into all seemly and generous arts and affairs ; till which in some measure be compassed, at mine own peril and cost, I refuse not to sustain this expectation from as many as are not loth to hazard so much credulity upon the best pledges that I can give them.". And when he came to redeem his pledge, in the very opening lines of his epic, trusting to the same inspiration, he challenges the supremacy of the ancients by his

> adventrous song
> That with no middle flight intends to soar
> Above the Aonian mount, while it pursues
> Things unattempted yet in prose or rhyme.

"This man cuts us all out, and the Ancients too," Dryden is reported to have said.   But this man intended to do no less, and formally announced his intention. It is impossible to outface Milton, or to abash him with praise. His most enthusiastic eulogists are compelled merely to echo the remarks of his earliest and greatest critic, himself. Yet with all this, none of the later critics, not the most cavalier nor the dullest, has dared to call him vain. His estimate of himself, offered as simple fact, has been accepted in the same spirit, and one abyss of ineptitude still yawns for the heroic folly, or the clownish courage, of the New Criticism.

CHAPTER I

JOHN MILTON

JOHN MILTON, the son of a middle-aged scrivener, was born on Friday, December the 9th, 1608, at his father's house in Bread Street, Cheapside ; and died on Sunday, November the 8th, 1674, in a small house, with but one room on a floor, in Artillery Walk, Bunhill Fields, London. Of his father the records that remain show him to have been a convinced member of the Puritan party in the Church, a man of liberal culture and intelligence, a lover of music (which taste Milton inherited), a wise and generous friend to the son who became a poet. We owe it to his wisdom rather than to his prosperity that Milton was allowed to live at home without any ostensible profession until he was thirty years of age and more.

For the first sixteen years of his life Milton was educated partly at home, by a Presbyterian tutor called Thomas Young, partly at St. Paul's

School, which he attended for some years as a day-scholar. From his twelfth year onward he was an omnivorous reader, and before he left school had written some boyish verses, void of merit. The next fourteen years of his life, after leaving school, were spent at Cambridge, in Buckinghamshire, and in foreign travel, so that he was thirty years old before he lived continuously in London again.

We know pretty well how he spent his time at Cambridge and at Horton, sedulously turning over the Greek and Latin classics, dreaming of immortality. We know less about his early years in London, where there were wider and better opportunities of gaining an insight into "all seemly and generous arts and affairs." London was a great centre of traffic, a motley crowd of adventurers and traders even in those days, and the boy Milton must often have wandered down to the river below London Bridge to see the ships come in. His poems are singularly full of figures drawn from ships and shipping, some of them bookish in their origin, others which may have been suggested by the sight of ships. Now it is Satan, who, after his fateful journey through chaos, nears the world,

> And like a weather-beaten vessel holds
> Gladly the port, though shrouds and tackle torn.

Now it is Dalila, whom the Chorus behold approaching

> Like a stately ship
> Of Tarsus, bound for the isles
> Of Javan or Gadire,
> With all her bravery on, and tackle trim,
> Sails filled, and streamers waving,
> Courted by all the winds that hold them play.

Or, again, it is Samson reproaching himself,

> Who, like a foolish pilot, have shipwracked
> My vessel trusted to me from above,
> Gloriously rigged.

The bulk of Satan is compared to the great sea-beast Leviathan, beheld off the coast of Norway by

> The pilot of some small night-founder'd skiff.

And in his approach to the happy garden the Adversary is likened to

> them who sail
> Beyond the Cape of Hope, and now are past
> Mozambic, off at sea north-east winds blow
> Sabaean odours from the spicy shore
> Of Araby the Blest, with such delay
> Well pleased they slack their course, and many a league
> Cheered with the grateful smell old Ocean smiles ;
> So entertained those odorous sweets the Fiend.

There is nothing here that is not within the reach of any inland reader, but Milton's choice of nautical similitudes may serve to remind us how much of the interest of Old London centred round its port. Here were to be heard those tales of far-sought adventure and peril which gave even

to the boisterous life of Elizabethan London an air
of triviality and security. Hereby came in "the
variety of fashions and foreign stuffs," which Fynes
Moryson, writing in Milton's childhood, compares
to the stars of heaven and the sands of the sea for
number. All sorts of characters, nationalities, and
costumes were daily to be seen in Paul's Walk,
adjoining Milton's school. One sort interests us
pre-eminently. "In the general pride of England,"
says Fynes Moryson, "there is no fit difference
made of degrees ; for very Bankrupts, Players,
and Cutpurses go apparelled like gentlemen."
Shakespeare was alive during the first seven years
of Milton's life, and was no doubt sometimes a
visitor to the Mermaid, a stone's throw from the
scrivener's house. Perhaps his cloak brushed the
child Milton in the street. Milton was born in
the golden age of the drama, and a score of
masterpieces were put upon the London stage
while he was in his cradle. But the golden age
passed rapidly ; the quality of the drama degener-
ated and the opposition to it grew strong before
he was of years to attend a play. Perhaps he
never saw a play by the masters during his boyhood, and his visits

> to the well-trod stage anon,
> If Jonson's learned sock be on,
> Or sweetest Shakespeare, Fancy's child,
> Warble his native woodnotes wild,

were either excursions of the imagination or belong
to his later occasional sojourns in London. In his
Eikonoklastes he quotes certain lines from *Richard
III.*, and here and there in his prose, as well as in
his verse, there are possibly some faint reminiscences
of Shakespearian phrases. So, for instance, in *The
Doctrine and Discipline of Divorce*, he seems to
echo a famous speech of Macbeth, while he claims
that his remedy of free divorce "hath the virtue to
soften and dispel rooted and knotty sorrows, and
without enchantment." But these are doubtless
the memories of reading. In the *Apology for
Smectymnuus*, when he has to reply to the charge
that he "haunted playhouses" during his college
days, he retorts the charge, it is true, rather than
denies it. Yet the retort bespeaks a certain
severity and preciseness in judging of plays and
their actors, which can hardly have found gratifica-
tion in the licenses and exuberances of the contemporary drama. It was not difficult, he remarks,
to see plays, "when in the Colleges so many of
the young divines, and those in next aptitude to
divinity, have been seen so often upon the stage,
writhing and unboning their clergy limbs to all
the antic and dishonest gestures of Trinculoes,
buffoons, and bawds." "If it be unlawful," he
continues, "to sit and behold a mercenary
comedian personating that which is least unseemly
for a hireling to do, how much more blameful is it

to endure the sight of as vile things acted by persons either entered, or presently to enter into the ministry ; and how much more foul and ignominious for them to be the actors! "

It was, at least, a happy chance that the first of Milton's verses to appear in print should have been *An Epitaph on the Admirable Dramatick Poet, W. Shakespeare*, contributed to the Second Folio in 1632. The main interests of the household at the Spread Eagle in Bread Street must have been far enough remote from the doings of the companies of players. John Milton the elder would probably have agreed with Sir Thomas Bodley, who called plays "riffe-raffes," and declared that they should never come into his library. The Hampton Court Conference, the Synod of Dort, the ever-widening divisions in the Church, between Arminian and Calvinist, between Prelatist and Puritan, were probably subjects of a nearer interest, even to the poet in his youth, than the production of new or old plays upon the stage. Milton's childhood was spent in the very twilight of the Elizabethan age ; it was greatly fortunate for him, and for us, that he caught the after-glow of the sunset upon his face. He read Spenser while Spenser was still the dominant influence in English poetry. "He hath confessed to me," said Dryden, "that Spenser was his original,"— an incredible statement unless we understand

"original" in the sense of his earliest admiration,
his poetic godfather who first won him to poetry.
He read Shakespeare and Jonson in the first
editions. He read Sylvester's translation of *Du
Bartas, His Divine Weekes and Workes;* and
perhaps thence conceived the first vague idea of a
poem on a kindred subject. It is necessary to
insist on his English masters, because, although the
greater part of his time and study was devoted to
the classics, the instrument that he was to use was
learned in a native school. His metre, his magnificent vocabulary, his unerring phraseology, took
learning and practice. He attached a high value
to his study of English poetry. When he spoke
of "our sage and serious Spenser (whom I dare be
known to think a better teacher than Scotus or
Aquinas)," he was conscious that he was maintaining what seemed a bold paradox in an age when
scholasticism still controlled education. It is
pleasant to think of Milton during these early
years, whether in London or at Christ's College,
in his "calm and pleasing solitariness, fed with
cheerful and confident thoughts," before ever he
had a hint that he must perforce "embark in a
troubled sea of noises and hoarse disputes, put
from beholding the bright countenance of truth in
the quiet and still air of delightful studies." From
the first, we may be sure, he read the poets as one
poet reads another, and apprenticed himself to

them for their craft. He was never drawn out of
the highroad of art by the minuter and more en-
tangling allurements of scholarship. In one of his
Divorce pamphlets he tells, with the inevitable
touch of pride, how he never could delight in long
citations, much less in whole traductions, " whether
it be natural disposition or education in me, or
that my mother bore me a speaker of what God
made mine own, and not a translator."

Milton was intended by his family, and by his own
early resolves, for the service of the Church. The
growing unrest, therefore, in matters ecclesiastical
during the early part of the seventeenth century
could not but affect him. The various parties and
tendencies in the Church of England had never,
since the Reformation, attained to a condition of
stable equilibrium. But the settlement under
Elizabeth was strengthened, and the parties bound
together for thirty years, by the ever-present fear
of Rome. When that fear was allayed, and the
menace that hung over the very existence of the
nation removed by the defeat of the Armada, the
differences within the Church broke out afresh, and
waxed fiercer every year. Shakespeare grew to
manhood during the halcyon years between the
Marian persecutions and the Marprelate pamphlets
—a kind of magic oasis, which gave us our
English Renaissance. Milton's youth breathed a
very different air. The Church, as it was, pleased

hardly any party. Much of the old temple had been hastily pulled down ; the new government offices that were to replace it had as yet been but partially built, and commanded no general approval. Considered as a social organisation, moreover, the Church throughout large parts of the country had fallen into a state not unlike decay. Richard Baxter, whose testimony there is no sufficient reason to reject, tells of its state in Shropshire during the years of his youth, from 1615 onwards :—" We lived in a country that had but little preaching at all : In the Village where I was born there was four Readers successively in Six years time, ignorant Men, and two of them immoral in their lives ; who were all my Schoolmasters.   In the Village where my Father lived, there was a Reader of about Eighty years of Age that never preached, and had two Churches about Twenty miles distant :   His Eyesight failing him, he said Common-Prayer without Book ; but for the Reading of the Psalms and Chapters he got a Common Thresher and Day-Labourer one year, and a Taylor another year : (for the Clerk could not read well) : And at last he had a Kinsman of his own (the excellentest Stage-player in all the Country, and a good Gamester and good Fellow) that got Orders and supplied one of his Places. . . . After him another Neighbour's Son took Orders, when he had been a while an Attorney's

Clerk, and a common Drunkard, and tipled himself
into so great Poverty that he had no other way to
live. . . . These were the School-masters of my
Youth . . . who read Common Prayer on Sun-
days and Holy Days, and taught School and
tipled on the Weekdays, and whipt the Boys when
they were drunk, so that we changed them very
oft. Within a few miles about us were near a
dozen more Ministers that were near Eighty years
old apiece, and never preached ; poor ignorant
Readers, and most of them of Scandalous Lives."
Some few there were, Baxter admits, who preached
in the neighbourhood, but any one who went to
hear them " was made the Derision of the Vulgar
Rabble under the odious Name of a *Puritane*."

In one of his Latin letters written from Cambridge, Milton himself speaks of the ignorance of
those designed for the profession of divinity, how
they knew little or nothing of literature and philosophy. The high prelacy and ritualism of Laud
on the one hand, the Puritan movement on the
other, each in some measure a protest against this
state of things, were at fierce variance with each
other, and Milton's ear, from his youth upward,
was " pealed with noises loud and ruinous." The
age of Shakespeare was irrecoverably past, and it
was impossible for any but a few imperturbable
Cyrenaics, like Herrick, to " fleet the time care-
lessly, as they did in the golden world." The

large indifference of Shakespeare to current politics
was impossible for Milton. " I had as lief be a
Brownist as a politician," said the folly of Sir
Andrew Aguecheek and the wisdom of Shakespeare. But now the Brownists and the politicians
had it their own way ; and Milton was something
of both.

His notable early poems, written at College and
during his retreat in Buckinghamshire, have therefore a singular interest and pathos. He was not
long for the world in which these poems move
with so ineffable a native grace. They are the
poems of his youth, instinct with the sensibility
of youth, and of a delicate and richly nurtured
imagination. But they are also the poems of an
age that was closing, and they have a touch of the
sadness of evening. " I know not," says Dr.
Johnson, speaking of *L'Allegro* and *Il Penseroso*,
" whether the characters are kept sufficiently apart.
No mirth can indeed be found in his melancholy,
but I am afraid that I always meet some melancholy in his mirth." It is true ; for both characters are Milton himself, who embodies in separate
poems the cheerful and pensive elements of his own
nature—and already his choice is made. There is
something disinterested and detached about his
sketches of the merriment which he takes part
in only as a silent onlooker, compared with the
profound sincerity of the lines—

And may at last my weary age
Find out the peaceful hermitage,
The hairy gown and mossy cell,
Where I may sit and rightly spell
Of every star that heaven doth shew,
And every herb that sips the dew,
Till old experience do attain
To something like prophetic strain.

The rising tide of political passion submerged
the solemn Arcadia of his early fancies. Like
Lycidas, he was carried far from the flowers and
the shepherds to visit "the bottom of the monstrous world." Hence there may be made a whole
index of themes, touched on by Milton in his
early poems, as if in promise, of which no fulfil-
ment is to be found in the greater poems of his
maturity. His political career under the Commonwealth is often treated, both by those who applaud
and by those who lament it, as if it were the
merest interlude between two poetic periods. It
was not so ; political passion dominates and in-
forms all his later poems, dictating even their
subjects. How was it possible for him to choose
King Arthur and his Round Table for the subject
of his epic, as he had intended in his youthful
days ; when chivalry and the spirit of chivalry had
fought its last fight on English soil, full in the
sight of all men, round the forlorn banner of King
Charles? The policy of Laud and Strafford kept
Milton out of the Church, and sent him into

retirement at Horton ; the same policy, it may be plausibly conjectured, had something to do with the change in the subject of his long-meditated epic. From the very beginning of the civil troubles contemporary events leave their mark on all his writings. The topical bias (so to call it) is very noticeable in many of the subjects tentatively jotted down by him on the paper that is now in the library of Trinity College, Cambridge. The corrupted clergy, who make so splendid and, as some think, so irrelevant an appearance in *Lycidas*, figure frequently, either directly or by implication, in the long list of themes.

Without misgiving or regret, when the time came, Milton shut the gate on the sequestered paradise of his youth, and hastened downward to join the fighters in the plain. Before we follow him we may well "interpose a little ease" by looking at some of the beauties proper to the earlier poems, and listening to some of the simple pastoral melodies that were drowned when the organ began to blow. *L'Allegro* is full of them—

> Sometimes, with secure delight,
> The upland hamlets will invite,
> When the merry bells ring round,
> And the jocund rebecks sound
> To many a youth and many a maid
> Dancing in the chequered shade,
> And young and old come forth to play
> On a sunshine holiday.

That is Merry England of Shakespeare's time.
But already the controversy concerning the *Book
of Sports* had begun to darken the air. Already
the Maypole, that "great stinking idol," as an
Elizabethan Puritan called it, had been doomed to
destruction. Some years before *L'Allegro* was
written, a bard, who hailed from Leeds, had
lamented its downfall in the country of his
nativity—

> Happy the age, and harmelesse were the dayes,
>   (For then true love and amity was found)
> When every village did a May-pole raise,
>   And Whitson Ales and May games did abound :
> And all the lusty Yonkers in a rout
> With merry Lasses danced the rod about ;
> Then friendship to their banquets bid the guests,
> And poor men far'd the better for their feasts.

The next verse recalls that scene in *The Winter's
Tale* where Shakespeare draws a vivid picture of
Elizabethan country merrymaking—

> The Lords of Castles, Mannors, Townes, and Towers
>   Rejoyc'd when they beheld the Farmers flourish,
> And would come down unto the Summer-Bowers
>   To see the Country gallants dance the Morrice,
> And sometimes with his tenant's handsome daughter
> Would fall in liking, and espouse her after
> Unto his Serving-man, and for her portion
> Bestow on him some farme, without extortion.

> Alas poore Maypoles, what should be the cause
>   That you were almost banish't from the earth ?

You never were rebellious to the lawes,
　Your greatest crime was harmelesse honest mirth ;
What fell malignant spirit was there found
To cast your tall *Piramides* to ground ?
.　　.　　.　　.　　.　　.

And you my native towne, which was of old,
　(When as thy Bon-fires burn'd and May-poles stood,
And when thy Wassell-cups were uncontrol'd)
　The Summer Bower of Peace and neighbourhood,
Although since these went down, thou ly'st forlorn,
By factious schismes and humours over-borne,
Some able hand I hope thy rod will raise,
That thou maist see once more thy happy daies.

The hopes of the bard of Leeds were fulfilled
at the Restoration. Merriment, of a sort, came
back to England ; but it found no congenial accept-
ance from Milton. The Court roysterers, the
Hectors, Nickers, Scourers, and Mohocks, among
whom were numbered Sedley and Rochester, and
others of the best poets of the day, are celebrated
by him incidentally in those lines, unsurpassable
for sombre magnificence, which he appends to his
account of Belial—

In courts and palaces he also reigns,
And in luxurious cities, where the noise
Of riot ascends above their loftiest towers,
And injury and outrage ; and, when night
Darkens the streets, then wander forth the sons
Of Belial, flown with insolence and wine.

The public festivals of these later days are
glanced at in *Samson Agonistes*—

> Lords are lordliest in their wine ;
> And the well-feasted priest then soonest fired
> With zeal, if aught religion seem concerned ;
> No less the people on their holy-days
> Impetuous, insolent, unquenchable.

There is no relaxation, no trace of innocent lightheartedness, in any of the later poems. Even the garden of Paradise, where some gentle mirth might perhaps be permissible, is tenanted by grave livers, majestic, but not sprightly. In *L'Allegro* the morning song of the milk-maid is "blithe," and the music of the village dance is "jocund." But Eve is described as "jocund" and "blithe" only when she is intoxicated by the mortal fruit of the tree ; and the note of gaiety that is heard faintly, like a distant echo, in the earlier poems, is never sounded again by Milton.

So it is also with other things. The flowers scattered on the laureate hearse of Lycidas make a brighter, more various, and withal a homelier display than ever meets the eye in the Hesperian wildernesses of Eden. Or take the world of fairy lore that Milton inherited from the Elizabethans —a world to which not only Shakespeare, but also laborious and arrogant poet-scholars like Jonson and Drayton had free right of entry. Milton, too, could write of the fairies—in his youth—

> With stories told of many a feat,
> How Faery Mab the junkets eat.

But even in *Comus* the most exquisite passage of
fairy description is put into the mouth of Comus
himself, chief of the band of ugly-headed monsters
in glistering apparel—

> The sounds and seas, with all their finny drove,
> Now to the moon in wavering morrice move ;
> And on the tawny sands and shelves
> Trip the pert fairies and the dapper elves.
> By dimpled brook and fountain-brim,
> The wood-nymphs decked with daisies trim,
> Their merry wakes and pastimes keep :
> What hath night to do with sleep ?

The song and the dance are broken off, never
to be resumed, when the staid footfall of the lady
is heard approaching. Milton cannot draw ugli-
ness ; it turns into beauty or majesty on his hands.
Satan has a large and enthusiastic party among
readers of *Paradise Lost*. Comus, we are told,
stands for a whole array of ugly vices—riot,
intemperance, gluttony, and luxury. But what a
delicate monster he is, and what a ravishing lyric
strain he is master of ! The pleasure that Milton
forswore was a young god, the companion of Love
and Youth, not an aged Silenus among the wine-
skins. He viewed and described one whole realm
of pagan loveliness, and then he turned his face the
other way, and never looked back. Love is of the
valley, and he lifted his eyes to the hills. His
guiding star was not Christianity, which in its

most characteristic and beautiful aspects had no fascination for him, but rather that severe and self-centred ideal of life and character which is called Puritanism. It is not a creed for weak natures ; so that as the nominal religion of a whole populace it has inevitably fallen into some well-merited disrepute. Puritanism for him was not a body of law to be imposed outwardly on a gross and timid people, but an inspiration and a grace that falls from Heaven upon choice and rare natures—

> Nor do I name of men the common rout,
> That, wandering loose about,
> Grow up and perish as the summer fly,
> Heads without name, no more remember'd ;

so sings the Chorus in *Samson Agonistes*—

> But such as thou hast solemnly elected,
> With gifts and graces eminently adorned,
> To some great work, thy glory,
> And people's safety, which in part they effect.

Under one form or another Puritanism is to be found in almost all religions, and in many systems of philosophy. Milton's Puritanism enabled him to combine his classical and Biblical studies, to reconcile his pagan and Christian admirations, Stoicism, and the Quakers. It was with no sense of incongruity that he gave to the Christ a speech in praise of—

> Quintus, Fabricius, Curius, Regulus, . . .
> Who could do mighty things, and could contemn
> Riches, though offered from the hand of Kings.

To reject common ambitions, to refuse common enticements, to rule passions, desires, and fears, " neither to change, nor falter, nor repent,"—this was the wisdom and this the virtue that he set before himself. There is no beatific vision to keep his eyes from wandering among the shows of earth. Milton's heaven is colder than his earth, the home of Titans, whose employ is political and martial. When his imagination deals with earthly realities, the noble melancholy of the Greeks lies upon it. His last word on human life might be translated into Greek with no straining and no loss of meaning—

> His servants He, with new acquist
> Of true experience from this great event,
> With peace and consolation hath dismissed,
> And calm of mind, all passion spent.

He is therefore one of the few English poets (alone in this respect among the greatest) who have not sung of Love. His only English love-poem, the sonnet *To the Nightingale*, is his earliest and poorest sonnet. He elected in his later poems to sing of Marriage, its foundation in reason, its utility, its respectability and antiquity as an institution, and, above all, its amazing dangers. He has thus lost the devotion of the young, who, while they read poetry by the ear and eye for its sonorous suggestions, and its processions of vague shapes, love Milton ; but when they come to read it for its matter and sentiment, leave him—in most cases never to return. The atmosphere of his later poems is that of some great public institution. Heaven is an Oriental despotism. Hell is a Secession parliament. In the happy garden itself there is no privacy, no individualism ; it is the focus of the action, the central point of the attack and the defence ; and a great part of the conversation of its inhabitants turns on the regulations under which they live. They never forget that they are all mankind, and when their psalm goes up in grateful adoration to their Creator, it is like the unanimous voice of all nations and kindreds and people and tongues.

"The plan of *Paradise Lost*," says Johnson, "has this inconvenience, that it comprises neither human actions nor human manners. The man and woman who act and suffer are in a state which no other man and woman can ever know. The reader finds no transaction in which he can be engaged ; beholds no condition in which he can by any effort of imagination place himself ; he has, therefore, little natural curiosity and sympathy." Milton, he goes on to explain, "knew human nature only in the gross, and had never studied the shades of character, nor the combinations of concurring or the perplexity of contending passions."

He knew human nature only in the gross. He treated nothing less momentous than the fortunes of the race. It is precisely from this cause that the incomparable grandeur of Milton's characters and situations springs. The conversations that he records are like international parleyings. Adam walks forth to meet the angel, in ambassadorial dignity, the accredited representative of the human race—

> Without more train
> Accompanied than with his own complete
> Perfections.; in himself was all his state,
> More solemn than the tedious pomp that waits
> On princes, when their rich retinue long
> Of horses led and grooms besmeared with gold
> Dazzles the crowd and sets them all agape.

And if the other characters of *Paradise Lost* have this generic stamp, it is because the chief character of all has it—the character of the poet himself. It lends a strange dignity to the story of Milton's life that in all his doings he felt himself to be a "cause," an agent of mighty purposes. This it is that more than excuses, it glorifies, his repeated magniloquent allusions to himself throughout the prose works. Holding himself on trust or on commission, he must needs report himself, not only to his great Taskmaster, but also from time to

time to men, his expectant and impatient bene-
ficiaries. Even in *Lycidas* he is thinking of
himself as much as of his dead companion—

> So may some gentle Muse
> With lucky words favour *my* destined urn,
> And as he passes turn,
> And bid fair peace be to my sable shroud.

What if he die young himself? Are his dreams
and hopes for his own future an illusion?
He agonises with the question in the famous
digression on poetry and poetic fame. But he
consoles himself by appeal to a Court where the
success and the fame of this world are as straw in
the furnace ; and then, having duly performed the
obsequies of his friend, with reinvigorated heart
he turns once more to the future—"To-morrow
to fresh woods and pastures new." A singular
ending, no doubt, to an elegy ! But it is blind
and hasty to conclude that therefore the precedent
laments are "not to be considered as the effusion
of real passion." A soldier's burial is not the less
honoured because his comrades must turn from
his grave to give their thought and strength and
courage to the cause which was also his. The
maimed rites, interrupted by the trumpet calling
to action, are a loftier commemoration than the
desolating laments of those who "weep the more
because they weep in vain." And in this way

Milton's fierce tirade against the Church hirelings, and his preoccupation with his own ambitions support and explain each other, and find a fit place in the poem. He is looking to his equipment, if perchance he may live to do that in poetry and politics, which Edward King had died leaving unaccomplished. When his own time came he desired to be lamented in no other way—

> Come, come ; no time for lamentation now,
> Nor much more cause. Samson hath quit himself
> Like Samson, and heroicly hath finished
> A life heroic, on his enemies
> Fully revenged.

This overmastering sense of the cause breathes through all his numerous references to himself. He stands in the Forum,

> Disturbed, yet comely, and in act
> Raised, as of some great matter to begin ;

and addresses himself, as he boasts in *The Second Defence of the People of England*, to "the whole collective body of people, cities, states, and councils of the wise and eminent, through the wide expanse of anxious and listening Europe." Having sacrificed the use of his eyes to the service of the commonweal, he bates not a jot of heart or hope—

> What supports me, dost thou ask ?
> The conscience, friend, to have lost them overplied
> In Liberty's defence, my noble task,
> Of which all Europe talks from side to side.

And while thus his fighting years are filled with
the exaltation of battle, as he plumes and lifts
himself upon the cause that is going forward, the
story of his closing years has in it much of the
pathos of a lost cause. It was remarked by
Johnson that there is in the *Paradise Lost* little
opportunity for the pathetic ; only one passage,
indeed, is allowed by him to be truly deserving of
that name. But the description of the remorse
and reconcilement of Adam and Eve, which
Johnson doubtless intended, will not compare, for
moving quality, with the matchless invocation to
the Seventh Book—

> More safe I sing with mortal voice, unchanged
> To hoarse or mute, though fallen on evil days,
> On evil days though fallen, and evil tongues,
> In darkness, and with dangers compassed round,
> And solitude ; yet not alone, while thou
> Visit'st my slumbers nightly, or when Morn
> Purples the East. Still govern thou my song,
> Urania, and fit audience find, though few.

Then the noise that he had heard, in imagination only, thirty years earlier, assails his bodily
ears ; as evening sets in, the wonted roar is up,
not in the wild woods of fancy inhabited by the
sensual magician and his crew, but in the unlighted
streets of Restoration London, as a chorus of cup-
shotten brawlers goes roaring by. The king is
enjoying his own again ; and the poet, hunted

and harassed in his last retreat, raises his petition
again to the Muse whom he had invoked at the
beginning of his task,—not Clio nor her sisters,
but the spirit of heavenly power and heavenly
wisdom ; his mind reverts to that story of Orpheus
which had always had so singular and personal
a fascination for him ; of Orpheus, who, holding
himself aloof from the mad amorists of Thrace,
was by them torn to pieces during the orgy of the
Dionysia, and sent rolling down the torrent of the
Hebrus ; and he prays to his goddess and
guardian—

> But drive far off the barbarous dissonance
> Of Bacchus and his revellers, the race
> Of that wild rout that tore the Thracian bard
> In Rhodope, where woods and rocks had ears
> To rapture, till the savage clamour drowned
> Both harp and voice ; nor could the Muse defend
> Her son.   So fail not thou, who thee implores ;
> For thou art heavenly, she an empty dream.

Disappointed of all his political hopes, living on
neglected and poor for fourteen years after the
Restoration, and dying a private citizen, passably
obscure, Milton yet found and took a magnanimous
revenge upon his enemies.   They had crippled
only his left hand in silencing the politician, but
his right hand, which had hung useless by his side
for so many years while he served the State, was
his own still, and wielded a more Olympian

weapon. In prose and politics he was a baffled man, but in poetry and vision he found his triumph. His ideas, which had gone a-begging among the politicians of his time, were stripped by him of the rags of circumstance, and cleansed of its dust, to be enthroned where they might secure a hearing for all time. The surprise that he prepared for the courtiers of the Restoration world was like Samson's revenge, in that it fell on them from above ; and, as elsewhere in the poem of *Samson Agonistes*, Milton was thinking not very remotely of his own case when he wrote that jubilant semi-chorus, with the marvellous fugal succession of figures, wherein Samson, and by inference Milton himself, is compared to a smouldering fire revived, to a serpent attacking a hen-roost, to an eagle swooping on his helpless prey, and last, his enemies now silent for ever, to the phœnix, self-begotten and self-perpetuating. The Philistian nobility (or the Restoration notables) are described, with huge scorn, as ranged along the tiers of their theatre, like barnyard fowl blinking on their perch, watching, not without a flutter of apprehension, the vain attempts made on their safety by the reptile grovelling in the dust below—

> But he, though blind of sight,
> Despised, and thought extinguished quite,
> With inward eyes illuminated,

His fiery virtue roused
From under ashes into sudden flame,
And as an evening dragon came,
Assailant on the perchèd roosts
And nests in order ranged
Of tame villatic fowl, but as an eagle
His cloudless thunder bolted on their heads.
So Virtue, given for lost,
Depressed and overthrown, as seemed,
Like that self-begotten bird
In the Arabian woods embost,
That no second knows nor third,
And lay erewhile a holocaust,
From out her ashy womb now teemed,
Revives, reflourishes, then vigorous most
When most unactive deemed ;
And, though her body die, her fame survives,
A secular bird, ages of lives.

CHAPTER II

It is customary for the friends of Milton to approach his prose works with a sigh of apology. There is a deep-rooted prejudice among the English people against a poet who concerns himself intimately with politics. Whether this feeling has its origin in solicitude for the poet or for the politics is hard to determine ; indeed it is pretty generally maintained that each is detrimental to the other. But seeing that for one man in the modern world who cares for poets there are at least ten who care for politics, it is safe to assume that the poets, when they are deprived of the franchise, are deprived rather to maintain the purity and efficiency of politics than for the good of their own souls. They have been compared to birds of Paradise, which were long believed to have no feet ; and the common sense of the English people, with a touch of the municipal logic of Dogberry, has enacted that whereas they have no feet, and have moreover been proved to have no feet, it shall be forbidden them, under the strictest pains and penalties, to alight and walk. Their function is to beautify the distant landscape with the flash of wings.

For most men common-sense is the standard, and immediate utility the end, whereby they judge political questions, great and small. Now common-sense judges only the questions that are brought home to it by instant example ; and utility is appealed to for a verdict only amid the dense crowd of actual conflicting interests. Neither the one nor the other is far-sighted or imaginative. So it comes about that the political system, in England, at least, is built up piecemeal ; it is founded on appetites and compromises, and mortared by immemorial habit. To explain this process, and to transfigure it in the pure light of imagination, was the work of the great poet-politician, Edmund Burke. But the poet usually goes a hastier way to work. Looking at the whole domiciliary structure from outside, he finds it shapeless and ugly, like an ant-heap ; and volunteers to play the architect. His design treats the details of individual habit and happiness in strict subordination to the desired whole. What he wants is consistency, symmetry, dignity ; and to achieve these he is willing to make a holocaust of human selfishnesses. He may be a deep scholar and thinker, but he is apt to forget one point of ancient wisdom,—that it is the wearer of the shoe, and not the cobbler, who best knows where the shoe wrings him.

The speculations of the poet awaken no hostile resentment so long as they are admittedly abstract. He is at liberty to build his Republic, his City of the Sun, his Utopia, or his New Atlantis, amid the indifferent applause of mankind. But when his aim becomes practical and immediate, when he seeks to stir the heap by introducing into it the ruthless discomfort of an idea, a million littlenesses assail him with deadly enmity, and he is found sorrowfully protesting his amazement :—

> I did but prompt the age to quit their clogs
> By the known rules of ancient liberty,
> When straight a barbarous noise environs me
> Of owls and cuckoos, asses, apes, and dogs.

So he is brought, with great reluctance, to the estimate of men which is expressed by Milton in *The Tenure of Kings and Magistrates ;* "being slaves within doors, no wonder that they strive so much to have the public state conformably governed to the inward vicious rule whereby they govern themselves. For indeed none can love freedom heartily but good men."

Milton cannot claim the exemption from censure which is allowed to the theorists, the builders of ideal states somewhere in the clouds. On his own behalf he expressly disclaims any such intention. "To sequester out of the world," he says, "into Atlantic and Utopian politics, which never can be drawn into use, will not mend our condition; but to ordain wisely as in this world of evil, in the midst whereof God has placed us unavoidably." Poetry might well have served him, if his object had been to add another to imaginary commonwealths. He took up with politics because he believed that in the disorder of the times his ideas might be made a "programme," and carried into effect.

It was in 1641, when already "the vigour of the Parliament had begun to humble the pride of the bishops," that he first intervened. "I saw," he says, "that a way was opening for the establishment of real liberty; that the foundation was laying for the deliverance of mankind from the yoke of slavery and superstition. . . . I perceived that if I ever wished to be of use, I ought at least not to be wanting to my country, to the church, and to so many of my fellow-Christians, in a crisis of so much danger; I therefore determined to relinquish the other· pursuits in which I was engaged, and to transfer the whole force of my talents and my industry to this one important object." So he wrote the treatise in two books, *Of Reformation in England, and the causes that hitherto have hindered it.* His later pamphlets are all similarly occasional in nature, written with a particular and definite object in view. In these he advocates as practicable and much-needed reforms, among other things, the establishment of a perpetual republic on the lines of an oligarchy; the abolition of bishops, religious ceremonials, liturgies, tithes, and, indeed, of all regular payment or salary given to ministers of religion; the supersession of universities and public schools by the erection of new academic institutions, combining the functions of both, "in every City throughout this Land"; the legalisation of free divorce; and the repeal of the ordinances compelling all books to be licensed. If he did not advocate, in any of the works put forth during his lifetime, the legal toleration of polygamy, it was probably only because he perceived that that, at least, did not fall within the scope of practical politics. He defends it in his posthumous treatise, *De Doctrinâ Christianâ*.

It will readily be seen that on almost all these questions Milton was not only—to use the foolish modern phrase—"in advance of his time," but also considerably in advance of ours. Twenty years after his death the Licensing Acts were abolished; for the rest, his reforms are yet to accomplish. It is an odd remark of one of his learned biographers that the *Areopagitica* is the only one of all Milton's prose writings "whose topic is not obsolete." It is the only one of his prose writings whose thesis commands the general assent of modern readers, and is, therefore, from his own practical point of view, obsolete. The mere enumeration of his opinions suffices to show that Milton's is a sad case of the poet in politics. The labours of the twenty prime years of his manhood have been copiously bewailed. To have Pegasus in harness is bad enough ; but when the waggon that he draws is immovably stuck in the mud, and he himself bespattered by his efforts, the spectacle is yet more pitiable. Many of his critics have expressed regret that he did not make for himself an artificial seclusion, and continue his purely poetical labours, with the classics for companions. The questions that drew him into politics were burning questions, it is true ; but were there not others to deal with them, good, earnest, sensible, homely people ? Samuel Butler has enumerated some of those who were dedicating their time and thought to politics at this important crisis :—

> The oyster-women locked their fish up,
> And trudged away to cry " No Bishop " :
> The mouse-trap men laid save-alls by,
> And 'gainst ev'l counsellors did cry ;
> Botchers left old cloaths in the lurch,
> And fell to turn and patch the Church ;
> Some cried the Covenant, instead
> Of pudding-pies and ginger-bread,

And some for brooms, old boots and shoes,
Bawled out to purge the Common-house :
Instead of kitchen-stuff, some cry
A gospel-preaching ministry ;
And some for old shirts, coats or cloak,
No surplices nor service-book ;
A strange harmonious inclination
Of all degrees to reformation.

But what was Milton doing in this malodorous
and noisy assembly?   Might he not with all confidence have left the Church to the oyster-women,
and the State to the mouse-trap men ?   The
company that he kept with them ruined his
manners ; he had to speak loud in order to be
heard, to speak broad in order to be respected ;
and so (bitterest thought of all!) he lost something of that sweet reasonableness which is a poet's
proper grace.

The answer to this strain of criticism is to be
found in the study of Milton's works, poetry and
prose—and perhaps best in the poetry.   We could
not have had anything at all like *Paradise Lost*
from a dainty, shy poet-scholar ; nor anything
half so great.   The greatest men hold their power
on this tenure, that they shall not husband it
because the occasion that presents itself, although
worthy of high effort, is not answerable to the re-
finement of their tastes.   Milton, it is too often
forgotten, was an Englishman.   He held the
privilege and the trust not cheap.   When God

intends some new and great epoch in human history, " what does he then," this poet exultantly asks, " but reveal himself to his servants, and, as his manner is, first to his Englishmen?" To his chief work in poetry he was instigated by patriotic motives. "I applied myself," he says, "to that resolution which Ariosto followed against the persuasions of Bembo, to fix all the industry and art I could unite to the adorning of my native tongue, not to make verbal curiosity the end (that were a toilsome vanity), but to be an interpreter and relater of the best and sagest things among mine own citizens throughout this island in the mother dialect."

There is plenty of "verbal curiosity" in Milton's poetry ; he is in some respects the finest craftsman who ever handled the English speech : so that this declaration is the more timely to remind us by how wide a chasm he is separated from those modern greenhouse poets who move contentedly in an atmosphere of art ideals and art theories. He had his breeding from the ancient world, where Æschylus fought at Marathon, and he could not think of politics as of a separable part of human life.

> To sport with Amaryllis in the shade,
> Or with the tangles of Neæra's hair,

is a lyric ideal that may quite well consist with

political indifference, but how should an epic inspiration be nourished where the prosperity of the
State is lightly esteemed ? Even had poetry lost
by his political adventures, he would have been
content that politics should gain. And politics
did gain ; for Milton's prose works raise every
question they touch, even where they cannot truly
be said to advance it. It is as unseemly for the
politicians to complain of his choice, as it would
be for the herdsmen of King Admetus to complain of the presence among them of a god. The
large considerations and high passions imported
into the treatment of practical questions by a
Milton, or a Burke, have done much to keep
even party politics at a high level in England, so
that civil servants and journalists may join in the
hymn of the herdsmen—

> He has been our fellow, the morning of our days,
> Us he chose for house-mates, and this way went.
>> God, of whom music
>> And song and blood are pure,
>> The day is never darkened
>> That had thee here obscure !

In a long autobiographic passage in the *Second
Defence of the People of England* Milton makes a
formal classification of his prose works written
before that date. All of them, he says, were
designed to promote Liberty. By the accidents
of the time he was induced to treat first, in his

anti - episcopal pamphlets, of religious liberty.
Once that controversy was fairly ablaze, in the
name of the same goddess he applied his incendiary
torch to humbler piles. "I perceived," he says,
" that there were three species of liberty which are
essential to the happiness of social life—religious,
domestic, and civil ; and as I had already written
concerning the first, and the magistrates were
strenuously active in obtaining the third, I determined to turn my attention to the second, or the
domestic species." He includes in this division of
his work the Divorce pamphlets, the tractate
Of Education, and the *Areopagitica*, as dealing with
the "three material questions" (so he calls them)
of domestic liberty, namely, "the conditions of the
conjugal tie, the education of the children, and the
free publication of the thoughts."

It seems a strange conception of domestic
liberty which makes it rest on a threefold support
—divorce at will, an unrestrained printing-press,
and the encyclopædic education of polyglot
children. But the truth is that Milton's classification is an after-thought. The pamphlets that
he names were all written by him much about the
same time, between 1643 and 1645 ; but the true
history of their origin is more interesting and less
symmetrical than the later invented scheme of
classification. The Divorce pamphlets were
written because Milton was unhappily married.

The *Areopagitica* was written because his heterodox views concerning marriage had brought him into collision with the Presbyterian censors of the press. His treatise on education was written because he had undertaken the education of his own nephews, and had become deeply interested in that question. In all three his own experience is the first motive ; in all three that experience is concealed beneath a formidable array of general considerations, dogmatically propounded.

The case is the same with regard to the pamphlets that treat of religious and civil liberty ; they are not only occasional, but intensely personal, even in their origins. The earliest of them, the five ecclesiastical pamphlets of the year 1641, deal with a question which had been of intimate concern to Milton ever since the beginning of his Cambridge days. The celebrated controversy with Salmasius and his abettors, concerning the death of King Charles, is a gladiatorial combat from which every element save the personal is often absent. In these bouts offensive biography and defensive autobiography serve for sword and shield. This personal character of the prose writings, while it has repelled some readers interested mainly in the questions discussed, has attracted others who are interested chiefly in the writer. A rich harvest of personal allusion has been gathered from the controversial treatises, and perhaps, even now, the

E

field has not been gleaned to the last ear. It is worthy of remark, for instance, how Milton's pre-occupation with the themes which he had already pondered, and turned this way and that in his mind, to test their fitness for a monumental work, shows itself in his choice of figure and allusion. Attention has often been called to the elaborate comparison, founded on the history of Samson, in *The Reason of Church Government urged against Prelaty* :—

"I cannot better liken the state and person of a king than to that mighty Nazarite Samson ; who being disciplined from his birth in the precepts and the practice of temperance and sobriety, without the strong drink of injurious and excessive desires, grows up to a noble strength and perfection with those his illustrious and sunny locks, the laws, waving and curling about his god-like shoulders. And while he keeps them about him undiminished and unshorn, he may with the jawbone of an ass, that is, with the word of his meanest officer, suppress and put to confusion thousands of those that rise against his just power. But laying down his head among the strumpet flatteries of prelates, while he sleeps and thinks no harm, they, wickedly shaving off all those bright and weighty tresses of his law, and just prerogatives, which were his ornament and strength, deliver him over to indirect and violent counsels, which, as those

Philistines, put out the fair and far-sighted eyes of
his natural discerning, and make him grind in the
prison-house of their sinister ends and practices
upon him : till he, knowing this prelatical rasor to
have bereft him of his wonted might, nourish
again his puissant hair, the golden beams of law
and right ; and they, sternly shook, thunder with
ruin upon the heads of those his evil counsellors,
but not without great affliction to himself."

This ingenious allegorical application naturally
finds no place in the grave poem of Milton's
latest years.   And yet, in one passage at least,
his earlier love for the high-figured style took
him captive again.   The strong drink from which
the Samson of the play abstains is strong drink,
not "injurious and excessive desires."   There is
no hint of prelatical conspiracy in the enticements
of Dalila.   But perhaps some faint reminiscence of
his earlier fable concerning Samson's hair recurred
to Milton's mind when he gave to Manoa a
speech comparing the locks of the hero to the
strength, not of the law, but of a nation in arms :—

> And I persuade me God had not permitted
> His strength again to grow up with his hair,
> Garrisoned round about him like a camp
> Of faithful soldiery, were not his purpose
> To use him further yet in some great service.

The theme of *Samson Agonistes* had thus already
taken possession of Milton's imagination when he

wrote his first prose tractates. But the same writings furnish even stronger evidence of his early dallyings with the theme of *Paradise Lost.* " It was from out the rind of one apple tasted," he says in the *Areopagitica,* "that the knowledge of good and evil, as two twins cleaving together, leaped forth into the world." And again, in *The Doctrine and Discipline of Divorce:*—"The academics and stoics . . . knew not what a consummate and most adorned Pandora was bestowed upon Adam, to be the nurse and guide of his arbitrary happiness and perseverance, I mean, his native innocence and perfection, which might have kept him from being our true Epimetheus." Some of these references show the imaginative scheme of the *Paradise Lost* in the process of building. In one passage, for instance, of the last quoted treatise, Milton expounds the pagan belief that God punishes his enemies most when he throws them furthest from him :—" Which then they held he did, when he blinded, hardened, and stirred up his offenders, to finish and pile up their desperate work since they had undertaken it. To banish for ever into a local hell, whether in the air or in the centre, or in that uttermost and bottomless gulf of chaos, deeper from holy bliss than the world's diameter multiplied, they thought not a punishing so proper and proportionate for God to inflict as to punish sin with sin." It would seem as if the poet had not as yet fixed the situation of his local hell, but remained suspended between rival theories.   The other idea, of the Divine permission and impulse given to hardened sinners, finds a conspicuous place in the poem.   In one instance, at least, a figure drawn from the story of the Creation is violently handled to serve strange uses.   The evolution of the four elements from the chaotic welter of hot, cold, moist, and dry, is adduced as a proof that the laws of God and of nature approve free divorce :—" By his divorcing command the world first rose out of chaos, nor can be renewed again out of confusion, but by the separating of unmeet consorts."

Allusions of this kind occur most frequently in the earlier prose writings, while the studies that had been interrupted by controversy were yet fresh in Milton's memory.   They would hardly be worth the quotation, were it not that they are another evidence of the transparency of his mind. In looking through his prose works you see traces of all that was engaging his imagination and thought at the time.   Poetry is the highest of expressive arts ; and poets are the worst dissemblers or economisers of truth in the world.   Their knowledge, like their feeling, possesses them, and must find expression as argument, or illustration, or figure, whatever the immediate matter in hand. The prose works of Milton are thus, from first to

last, an exposition of himself. The divorce
pamphlets, especially, are hot with smothered
personal feeling. Long years afterwards, when
time and change had softened and blurred it in
memory, his early misadventure was reflected in
more than one passage of the later poems. The
humble plaint of Eve, and the description of her
reunion with her alienated lord, in the Tenth Book
of *Paradise Lost*, doubtless contains, as has often
been said, some reflection of what took place at a
similiar interview in 1645, when Mistress Mary
Milton returned to her offended husband. That
one principal cause of the rupture has been rightly
divined, by Mr. Mark Pattison and others, is
probable from certain remarkable lines in the
Eighth Book, where Adam describes how he was
presented with his bride :—

On she came,
Led by her Heavenly Maker, though unseen,
And guided by his voice, nor uninformed
Of nuptial sanctity, and marriage rites.

Even at so wide a remove of time, the poet's
wounded pride finds expression in this singular
theory—or, rather, in this more than dubious piece
of self-justification.

But although the hurt he had suffered, in his
most susceptible feelings, gives eloquence and
plangency to his divorce pamphlets, it was not
merely to voice his sufferings that he wrote those

pamphlets. Most men in Milton's position, married to " a nothing, a desertrice, an adversary," would have recognised that theirs was one of those exceptional cases for which the law cannot provide, and would have sat down under their unhappy chance, to bear it or mitigate it as best they might. Some poets of the time of the Romantic Revival would have claimed the privilege of genius to be a law unto itself ; the law of the State being designed for the common rout, whose lesser sensibilities and weaker individuality make them amenable to its discipline. Milton did neither the one thing nor the other. The modern idolatry of genius was as yet uninvented ; he was a citizen first, a poet and an unhappy man afterwards. He directed his energies to proving, not that he should be exempted from the operation of the law, but that the law itself should be changed. He had entered into marriage, with full ceremonial ushering, by the main door ; he would go out the same way, or not at all. Thus even in this most personal matter he pleads, not for himself, but for the commonweal. He cannot conceive of happiness as of a private possession, to be secretly enjoyed ; it stands rooted, like justice, in the wise and equal ordinances of the State ; and the only freedom that he values is freedom under the law.

Like the citizen of some antique state, he discourses of marriage in the market-place. In his efforts to be persuasive, both here and in the *Areopagitica*, he humbles himself to management and the seasonings of flattery. It is a new trade for him, and suits oddly with his pride. But he hoped much, at this time, from the Parliament, that "select assembly," containing so many "worthy senators" and "Christian reformers," "judges and lawgivers." In the enthusiasm of his hopes, he credits them with a desire "to imitate the old and elegant humanity of Greece," with a wisdom greater than that of the Athenian Parliament, with a magnanimous willingness to repeal their own acts at the dictate of the voice of reason. And all this at a time when the Presbyterians were in the ascendant, intent upon establishing a discipline neither old, nor elegant, nor humane, so little acquainted with Greece, that it was one of Selden's amusements to confute their divines by citing a reading from the Greek Testament. Milton was destined to grievous disappointment, and his rage against the Presbyterians, in some of his later pamphlets, was the fiercer.

But although his pamphlets are both occasional and personal, and even address themselves at times to conciliation and persuasion, the views that they advocate and the system of thought that underlies them were not the products of time and accident. Milton was an idealist, pure and simple,

in politics. Had he lived under the Tudor
sovereigns, he would have been reduced, with Sir
Thomas More, Montaigne, and John Barclay, the
author of *Argenis*, to express himself by way of
romance and allegory. It was his fortune to live
at a time when the Tudor state system was breaking
up with appalling suddenness, and along with it the
Tudor compromise in the affairs of the Church,
imposed from above upon an unawakened people,
was falling into wreckage. Here was an opportunity that has not often, in the world's history,
come to a poet, of realising the dream that he
had dreamed in his study, of setting up again, for
the admiration and comfort of posterity, the model
of an ancient Republic.

The best of all Milton's critics has left us the
worst account of his political opinions. Johnson's
censure of *Lycidas*, much as it has been ridiculed
and decried, is judicious and discerning compared
with his explanation of Milton's political creed :—
" Milton's republicanism was, I am afraid, founded
in an envious hatred of greatness, and a sullen
desire of independence, in petulance impatient of
control, and pride disdainful of superiority. He
hated monarchs in the State, and prelates in the
Church ; for he hated all whom he was required to
obey. It is to be suspected that his predominant
desire was to destroy, rather than establish, and
that he felt not so much the love of liberty as

repugnance to authority." It may, at least, be credited to Johnson for moderation, that he requires only four of the Seven Deadly Sins, to wit, Pride, Envy, Anger, and Sloth, to explain Milton's political tenets. Had he permitted himself another sentence, an easy place might surely have been made for Gluttony, Luxury, and Covetousness, the three whose absence cannot fail to be remarked on by any lover of thorough and detailed treatment in these intricate problems of human character.

If, in our more modern fashion, we seek for the origin of Milton's ideas in his education, his habits of thought, and his admirations, we shall be obliged to admit that they are all rooted in his conception of the ancient City State. It was the wish of Thomas Hobbes to abolish the study of Greek and Latin in our schools and colleges, because this study fosters a love of freedom, and unfits men to be the subjects of an absolute monarch. His happiest illustration would have been the case of his contemporary, Milton. Yet in all Milton's writings there is no trace of the modern democratic doctrine of equality. A hearing is all that he claims. So far from hating greatness, he carries his admiration for it, for personal virtue and prowess, almost to excess. The poet who described the infernal conclave in the Second Book of *Paradise Lost* was not likely to be insensible to the part played in politics by men of eminent and dominating personality. To think of free government as of an engine for depressing unusual merit was impossible for Milton. He lived in an age that had found in Plutarch's men its highest ideals of political character. Never, since their own day, had the "noble Grecians and Romans" exercised so irresistible a fascination on the minds of men, or so real an influence on the affairs of the State, as was theirs at the time of the Renaissance. The mist in which they had long been enveloped was swept away, and these colossal figures of soldiers, patriots, and counsellors loomed large and clear across the ages, their majesty enhanced by distance and by art, which conspire to efface all that is accidental, petty, and distracting. We cannot see these figures as they appeared to the Renaissance world. One of the chief results of modern historical labour and research has been that it has peopled the Middle Ages for us, and interposed a whole society of living men, our ancestors, between us and ancient Rome. But in Milton's time this process was only beginning ; the collections and researches that made it possible were largely the work of his contemporaries, — and were despised by him. When he looked back on the world's history, from his own standpoint, he saw, near at hand and stretching away into the distance, a desert, from which a black mass of cloud had just been lifted ;

and, across the desert, lying fair under the broad
sunshine, a city—

> With gilded battlements, conspicuous far,
> Turrets and terrasses, and glittering spires.

It was towards this ancient civic life, with its
arts and arms and long renown, that he reached
forth passionate hands of yearning. The interven-
ing tract, whither his younger feet had wandered,
almost ceased to exist for him ; the paladins and
ladies of mediæval story were the deceitful mirage
of the desert ; the true life of antiquity lay beyond.
In all his allusions to the great themes of romance
two things are noticeable : first, how deeply his
imagination had been stirred by them, so that they
are used as a last crown of decoration in some of
the most exalted passages of his great poems ; and
next, how careful he is to stamp them as fiction.
His studies for the early *History of Britain* had
cloyed him with legends conveyed from book to
book. Once convinced that no certain historical
ground could be found for the feet among the
whole mass of these traditions, Milton ceased to
regard them as eligible subjects for his greatest
poem. But their beauty dwelt with him ; the
memory of the embattled chivalry of Arthur and
Charlemagne recurs to him when he is seeking for
the topmost reach of human power and splendour
that he may belittle it by the side of Satan's rebel

host ; and the specious handmaidens who served
the Tempter's phantom banquet in the desert are
described as lovely beyond what has been

> Fabled since
> Of fairy damsels met in forest wide
> By Knights of Logres, or of Lyones,
> Lancelot, or Pelleas, or Pellenore.

If Milton's attitude to mediæval romance is one
of regretful suspicion, his attitude to the greatest of
mediæval institutions is one of bitter contempt.
He inveighs even against the " antiquitarians,"
such as Camden, who, he says, " cannot but love
bishops as well as old coins and his much lamented
monasteries, for antiquity's sake." For near
twelve hundred years these same bishops " have
been in England to our souls a sad and doleful
succession of illiterate and blind guides." It is
needless to multiply extracts illustrative of Milton's
opinions on the Church ; behind the enormous
wealth of rhetoric and invective poured forth in
his pamphlets, the opinions that he holds are few
and simple. When he had been disappointed by
the Presbyterians, and had finally turned from them,
his beliefs inclined more and more, in two points
at least, to the tenets of the newly arisen sect of
Quakers—to a pure spiritualism in religion, and
the complete separation of Church and State.
Their horror of war he never shared. The model
of the Church he sought in the earliest records of

Christianity, and less and less even there ; the model of the State in the ancient republics. All subsequent experience and precedent was to him a hindrance and a mischief. So rapidly and easily does his mind leap from the ancient to the modern world, that even when he speaks of his love for the drama, as in his first Latin elegy or in *Il Penseroso*, it is sometimes difficult to say whether he is thinking of the Elizabethan or of the Attic dramatists.

The lodestar of his hopes is liberty, his main end the establishment of "a free commonwealth." He knows as well as Montesquieu that democracy in its pristine dignity can be erected only on a wide foundation of public virtue. " To govern well," he declares in the treatise *Of Reformation in England*, "is to train up a nation in true wisdom and virtue, and that which springs from thence, magnanimity (take heed of that), and that which is our beginning, regeneration, and happiest end, likeness to God, which in one word we call godliness ; . . . other things follow as the shadow does the substance." In the same pamphlet this envious hater of greatness remarks that " to govern a nation piously and justly, which only is to say happily, is for a spirit of the greatest size, and divinest mettle." And men worthy of this description had, as it seemed to him, arisen in his own time. His praise of Cromwell and the leaders associated with him is almost extravagant

in its enthusiasm. "While you, O Cromwell, are
left among us, he hardly shows a proper confidence
in the Supreme, who distrusts the security of
England, when he sees that you are in so special
a manner the favoured object of the Divine regard." His mind is full of the achievements of
Cyrus, Epaminondas, and Scipio ; he denies to
the Protector no honour that may be drawn from
these high comparisons. And then, as in *Lycidas*,
so also in *The Second Defence of the People of
England*, Milton concludes his celebration of
another by a return to himself and his pride in
a duty fulfilled. Opportunity, he declares, is
offered for great achievements ; if it be not
seized, posterity will judge "that men only
were wanting for the execution ; while they were
not wanting who could rightly counsel, exhort,
inspire, and bind an unfading wreath of praise
round the brows of the illustrious actors in so
glorious a scene."

In the measures that he recommends to Cromwell as necessary for the public welfare, his mis-
takes are the generous errors of an idealist. He
writes as if all were either Cromwells or Miltons,
and worthy of the fullest measure of liberty.
"Now the time seems come," he exclaims,
"wherein Moses, the great prophet, may sit in
heaven rejoicing to see that memorable and
glorious wish of his fulfilled, when not only our

seventy elders, but all the Lord's people, are become prophets." His general propositions on the function of law are unimpeachable. "He who wisely would restrain the reasonable soul of man within due bounds, must first himself know perfectly how far the territory and dominion extends of just and honest liberty. As little must he offer to bind that which God hath loosened as to loosen that which He hath bound. The ignorance and mistake of this high point hath heaped up one huge half of all the misery that hath been since Adam." But with the application to issues of the day it appears that the mistake has been all one way. "Laws are usually worse in proportion as they are more numerous." The free spirit of man can govern him without "a garrison upon his neck of empty and over-dignified precepts."

Whether he treat of religion, of education, of divorce, or of civil government, the error is always the same, a confidence too absolute in the capacity and integrity of the reasonable soul of man. A liturgy, for example, is intolerable, because it is a slur upon the extemporary effusions of ministers of the Gospel. "Well may men of eminent gifts set forth as many forms and helps to prayer as they please; but to impose them on ministers lawfully called and sufficiently tried . . . is a supercilious tyranny, impropriating the Spirit of God to themselves." Milton, we know, did not habitually attend public worship at any of the conventicles of the sectaries, or perhaps he might have found reason to modify this censure.

Some of his impassioned pleadings were possibly not wholly without effect on the politics of the time. It is interesting, at any rate, to find Cromwell, in his letter written in 1650 to the Governor of Edinburgh Castle, adopting one of the main arguments of the *Areopagitica*, and enforcing it against the Presbyterians by a figure which may have been borrowed from that tract. "Your pretended fear," he writes, "lest error should step in, is like the man who would keep all wine out of the country lest men should be drunk. It will be found an unjust and unwise jealousy to deprive a man of his natural liberty upon a supposition that he may abuse it. When he doth abuse it, judge." But Cromwell never applied his logic to the removal of the restraint upon printing, which by this same argument Milton had judged to be "the greatest displeasure and indignity to a free and knowing spirit that can be put upon him." He was too practical a statesman to be frightened into logic by a little paper shot.

Logical Milton always was. He learned little or nothing from the political events of his time. He was throughout consistent with himself; prepared to take any risks that his advocacy

F

might bring upon him, not prepared to forego or modify his opinions because of human incompetence or human imbecility. Between the consistent and unflinching Royalists on the one hand, and the consistent and unflinching Republicans on the other, the most of the population of England wavered and hung. But half-measures and half-heartedness were alike unintelligible to Milton. He fell upon the Presbyterians when they showed a disposition to palter with the logical consequences of their own action, and scourged them unmercifully. They had "banded and borne arms against their king, divested him, disanointed him, nay, cursed him all over in their pulpits, and their pamphlets." But when once the king was brought to trial, then "he who but erewhile in the pulpits was a cursed tyrant, an enemy to God and saints, laden with all the innocent blood spilt in three kingdoms, and so to be fought against, is now, though nothing penitent or altered from his first principles, a lawful magistrate, a sovereign lord, the Lord's anointed, not to be touched, though by themselves imprisoned." He prepares for them a similar dilemma, between the horns of which they have since been content to dwell, in his treatment of the question of divorce : "They dare not affirm that marriage is either a sacrament or a mystery . . . and yet they invest it with such an awful sanctity, and give it such adamantine chains to bind with, as if it were to be worshipped like some Indian deity, when it can confer no blessing upon us, but works more and more to our misery."

Milton's astonishment and indignation in cases like these are a convincing evidence of his inability to understand average politics, and that world of convenience, precaution, and compromise which is their native place. His own tenacity and constancy have something grim about them. Andrew Marvell, in his tract called *The Rehearsal Transprosed*, speaking of the intolerance of his adversary, Samuel Parker, says : "If you have a mind to die, or to be of his party (there are but these two conditions), you may perhaps be rendered capable of his charity." Neither of these two conditions was a certain title to the charity of Milton. In the *Eikonoklastes* he pursues the dead king with jibe and taunt, and exults over the smallest advantage gained. The opening words of the tract show him conscious of the difficulty and delicacy of the part he acted in making war on one who had "paid his final debt to nature and his faults." But what then? If the king, being dead, could speak, the dead king must be answered, and his gauntlet taken up "in the behalf of liberty and the commonwealth."

The manner in which he conducts this and

other controversies has brought upon Milton's head universal reproach. He is intemperate and violent, he heaps up personal scurrilities against his adversaries, and triumphs in their misfortunes. There is nothing wherein our age more differs from his than in the accepted rules governing controversy, and he has lost estimation accordingly. Yet not a few critics, it may be suspected, have allowed their dislike of the thing he says to hurry them into an exaggerated censure on his manner of saying it. It is important, in the first place, to remember that his violences are not the violences of the hired rhetorician. He was prepared to stand by what he wrote, and he knew the risks that he ran in those shifting and uncertain times. His life was in danger at the Restoration, and was saved by some unknown piece of good fortune or clemency. He was not a coward reviler, a " tongue-doughty giant," whose ears are the most delicate part about him, but an open fighter, who got as good as he gave. And then it is sometimes forgotten that the most scurrilous of Milton's pamphlets were written in Latin, a language which has always enjoyed an excellent liberty in the matter of personal abuse ; while even his English pamphlets, wherein at times he shows almost as pretty a talent in reviling, were written for an audience inured to the habitual amenities of Latin controversy. Sir Thomas

More was famous for his knack of calling bad names in good Latin, yet his posterity rise up and call him blessed. Milton, like More, observed the rules of the game, which allowed practices condemned in the modern literary prize-ring. He calls Salmasius a poor grammarian, a pragmatical coxcomb, a silly little scholar, a mercenary advocate, a loggerhead, a hare-brained blunderbuss, a witless brawler, a mongrel cur ; he reproaches him with the domestic tyranny put upon him by that barking she-wolf, his wife, and winds up with an elaborate comparison (not wholly unfamiliar to modern methods of controversy) between Salmasius and Judas. With his nameless opponent in the Divorce quarrel he deals — this time in English — no less contemptuously : " I mean not to dispute philosophy with this pork, who never read any." The creature is a conspicuous gull, an odious fool, a dolt, an idiot, a groom, a rank pettifogger, a presumptuous losel, a clown, a vice, a huckster-at-law, whose "jabberment is the flashiest and the fustiest that ever corrupted in such an unswilled hogshead." " What should a man say more to a snout in this pickle? What language can be low and degenerate enough? " In the *Apology* for Smectymnuus, Milton sets forth his own defence of his acrimony and violence : " There may be a sanctified bitterness," he remarks, "against the enemies of the

truth ; " and he dares to quote the casuistry of
Electra in *Sophocles* :—

> 'Tis you that say it, not I. You do the deeds,
> And your ungodly deeds find me the words.

The exigencies of controversy revealed in
Milton not only an inexhaustible store of coarse
invective, but also, at times, the flash of real wit.
" My fate," he says, with some sense of the incongruity of the thing, " extorts from me a talent of
sport, which I had thought to hide in a napkin."
We are privileged to hear Milton laugh. It is
not mirthful nor gentle laughter, but rather the
fierce, harsh, vehement laughter of the Hebrew
Psalms, the laughter of scorn, the shooting out of
the lips, the saying " Ha, ha." He speaks with
his mouth, and swords are in his lips. Thus, of
Alexander Morus, Professor of Sacred History at
Amsterdam, whom he suspected to be the author
of a tract in support of Salmasius, he says : " There
is one More, part Frenchman and part Scot, so
that one country or one people cannot be quite
overwhelmed with the whole infamy of his extrac-
tion " ; and he indulges himself in a debauch of
punning on *Morus*, the Latin word for a mulberry.
In the prelatical controversy, after discussing with
his opponent the meaning of the word " angel," he
continues : " It is not ordination nor jurisdiction
that is angelical, but the heavenly message of the

Gospel, which is the office of all ministers alike.
. . . And if you will contend still for a superiority
in one person, you must ground it better than
from this metaphor, which you may now deplore
as the axe-head that fell into the water, and say,
' Alas, master ! for it was borrowed ' ; unless you
have as good a faculty to make iron swim, as you
had to make light froth sink." In the *Apology*
for Smectymnuus he heaps one grotesque comparison on another. His adversary, the son of
Bishop Hall, is like "some empiric of false
accusations to try his poisons upon me, whether
they would work or not." The learning that was
displayed by the champion of Episcopacy and the
very typographical arrangement of his book incur
an equal contempt : the margin of his treatise "is
the sluice most commonly that feeds the drought
of his text. . . . Nor yet content with the wonted
room of his margin, but he must cut out large
docks and creeks into his text, to unlade the
foolish frigate of his unseasonable authorities."
His best folios " are predestined to no better end
than to make winding-sheets in Lent for pilchers."
With this last stroke Milton is so well pleased
that he repeats the same prediction in an elaborated
form over the works of Salmasius, and even cele-
brates in numerous verse the forethought and
bounty of one who has thus taken pity on the
nakedness of fishes.

The fantastic nature of these quips and taunts reminds us that Milton belonged to the age of the metaphysical poets and satirists, the age of Cowley, and Cleveland, and Butler. His prose works have been searched chiefly for passages that may be used to illustrate his poetry ; and although the search has been rewarded with many natural coincidences of expression, not a few passages of lofty self-confidence, and some raptures of poetic metaphor, the result has been in the main a disappointment. His admirers, too jealous for the poetic dignity of their hero, have turned away sorrowfully from this memorial heap of odd-shaped missiles, hurled from his dire left hand for the confusion of his enemies. And yet, rightly judged, there is instruction, and an increased reverence for the poet, to be found in these also— in all that wild array of subjects and methods which he commands for the purposes of his prose, but dismisses from the service of his verse. It was a strict and rare selection that he made among the auxiliaries when he addressed himself to the more arduous attempt. Here and there, even in *Paradise Lost*, his education in the handling of satire and invective stood him in stead. The poem contains more than one " flyting "—to use the Scottish term—and the high war of words between Satan and Abdiel in heaven, or between Satan and Gabriel on earth, could not have been

handled save by a master of all the weapons of
verbal fence and all the devices of wounding
invective. In the great close of the Fourth Book,
especially, where the arch-fiend and the archangel
retaliate defiance, and tower, in swift alternate
flights, to higher and higher pitches of exultant
scorn, Milton puts forth all his strength, and
brings into action a whole armoury of sarcasm and
insult whetted and polished from its earlier prosaic
exercise. Even the grotesque element in his
humour is not wholly excluded from the *Paradise
Lost;* it has full scope, for once, in the episodical
description of the Paradise of Fools—that barren
continent, beaten on by the storms of chaos, dark
save for some faint glimmerings from the wall of
heaven, the inhabitants a disordered and depraved
multitude of philosophers, crusaders, monks, and
friars, blown like leaves into the air by the winds
that sweep those desert tracts. Unlike the
Paradise that was lost, this paradise is wholly of
Milton's invention, and is the best extant monument to that spirit of mockery and savage triumph
which is all the humour that he knows.

The style of his prose works is a style formed
upon oratorical models. The long winding
sentence, propped on epithets and festooned with
digressions, was the habitual vehicle of his
meaning. The effect it produces at its best was
well described by Marvell, who, in a letter to

Milton thanking him for a copy of the *Defence of the People of England*, remarks : " When I consider how equally it turns and rises with so many figures, it seems to me a Trajan's column, in whose winding ascent we see embossed the several monuments of your learned victories." The clink of the rhyming couplet was not more displeasing to Milton's ear than the continued emphatic bark of a series of short sentences. Accustomed as he was to the heavy-armed processional manner of scholarly Renaissance prose, he felt it an indignity to " lie at the mercy of a coy, flirting style ; to be girded with frumps and curtal jibes, by one who makes sentences by the statute, as if all above three inches long were confiscate." Later on in the *Apology* he returns to this grievance, and describes how his adversary " sobs me out half a dozen phthisical mottoes, wherever he had them, hopping short in the measure of convulsion fits ; in which labour the agony of his wit having escaped narrowly, instead of well-sized periods, he greets us with a quantity of thumb-ring posies." The men of the Renaissance despised the homely savour of the native English syntax with its rude rhetoric and abrupt logic and its lore of popular adages and maxims ; they had learned to taste a subtler pleasure in the progressive undulations of a long mobile sentence, rising and falling alternately, reaching the limit of its height towards the middle, and at the close either dying away or breaking in a sudden crash of unexpected downward emphasis. This is the sentence preferred by Milton, and, where haste or zeal does not interfere with the leisurely ordering, handled by him with excellent skill. At its best and at its worst alike his prose is the prose of a poet. His sentences rarely conform to any strict periodic model ; each idea, as it occurs to him, brings with it a train of variation and enrichment, which, by the time the sentence closes, is often found in sole possession. The architecture depends on melody rather than logic. The emphasis and burden of the thought generally hangs on the epithets, descriptive terms, and phrases, which he strengthens by arranging them in pairs, after a fashion much practised by poets. Thus, to take a few examples from the Divorce pamphlets, a wife, who should be " an intimate and speaking help," " a ready and reviving associate," to comfort " the misinformed and wearied life of man " with " a sweet and gladsome society," is too often " a mute and spiritless mate," united to her husband in " a disconsolate and unenjoined matrimony," whereby the blessing that was expected with her is changed " into a familiar and coinhabiting mischief, at least into a drooping and disconsolate household captivity, without refuge or redemption." " The mystical and blessed union of marriage can be no way more unhallowed and profaned, than by the forcible uniting of such disunions and separations." "And it is a less breach of wedlock to part with wise and quiet consent betimes, than still to foil and profane that mystery of joy and union with a polluting sadness and perpetual distemper."

The balance of epithet, the delicate music, the sentence that resembles a chain with link added to link rather than a hoop whose ends are welded together by the hammer—these are the characteristics of Milton's prose. They are illustrated in that short passage of the *Areopagitica*, well known to all readers of English : " I cannot praise a fugitive and cloistered virtue, unexercised and unbreathed, that never sallies out and seeks her adversary, but slinks out of the race, where that immortal garland is to be run for, not without dust and heat." Or in the striking description of London during the Civil War : " Behold now this vast city, a city of refuge, the mansion-house of liberty, encompassed and surrounded with his protection ; the shop of war hath not there more anvils and hammers working, to fashion out the plates and instruments of armed justice in defence of beleaguered truth, than there be pens and heads there, sitting by their studious lamps, musing, searching, revolving new notions and ideas wherewith to present, as with their homage and their fealty, the approaching reformation ; others as fast reading, trying all things, assenting to the force of reason and convincement."

This sonorous balance of phrase and epithet cannot always escape what Milton himself calls "the heathenish battology of multiplying words." It serves the uses of rhetoric rather than of logic, and by the fervour of its repetitions and enlargements unfits his prose for the plainer purposes of argument or exposition. His argument is sometimes destroyed or blemished by the fire that it kindles, his narrative overwhelmed in the tide of passions that it sways.

His vocabulary is extraordinarily rich, and here again the contrast is great between his prose and his verse. A full-bodied and picturesque dictionary could be made of the words that occur only in the prose. Most of these words would be found to derive from the Saxon stock, which yields him almost all his store of invective and vituperation. The resources of his Latinised vocabulary enable him to rise by successive gyrations to a point of vantage above his prey, and then the downward rush that strikes the quarry is a Saxon monosyllable. In this cardinal point of art for those who have to do with the English speech he became the teacher of Burke, who, with a lesser wealth of Saxon at his command, employed it with a more telling parsimony.

Milton avoids no word of humble origin, so it serve his purpose. His contempt finds voice in such expressions as to "huddle" prayers, and to "keck" at wholesome food. Gehazi "rooks" from Naaman; the bishops "prog and pander for fees," and are "the common stales to countenance every politic fetch that was then on foot." The Presbyterians were earnest enough "while pluralities greased them thick and deep"; the gentlemen who accompanied King Charles in his assault on the privileges of the House of Commons were "the spawn and shipwreck of taverns and dicing-houses." The people take their religion from their minister "by scraps and mammocks, as he dispenses it in his Sunday's dole"; and "the superstitious man by his good will is an atheist, but being scared from thence by the pangs and gripes of a boiling conscience, all in a pudder shuffles up to himself such a God and such a worship as is most agreeable to remedy his fear."

There were few incidents in Milton's career, from his personal relations with his college tutor to his choice of blank verse for his epic, that he was not called upon at some time or other in his life to explain and defend. When his free use of homely figures and turns of speech was objected to him, his answer was ready : "Doth not Christ Himself teach the highest things by the similitude of old bottles and patched clothes ? Doth He not illustrate best things by things most evil ? His own coming to be as a thief in the night, and the righteous man's wisdom to that of an unjust steward ? " But the defence is misleading, for the rules that governed Milton's usage are not what it would suggest. When he came to treat of the best and highest things his use of native English became more sparing and dainty, while the rank, strong words that smack of the home soil were all foregone.

His prose works, therefore, help us to appreciate better the tribulations of the process whereby he became a classic poet. Eclecticism and the severe castigation of style are dangerous disciplines for any but a rich temperament ; from others. they produce only what is exquisite and thin and vapid. The " stylist " of the modern world is generally an interesting invalid ; his complexion would lose all its transparency if it were exposed to the weather ; his weak voice would never make itself heard in the hubbub of the bazaar. Sunbeams cannot be extracted from cucumbers, nor can the great manner in literature emanate from a chill self-culture. But Milton inherited the fulness and vigour of the Elizabethans, and so could afford to write an epic poem in a selection of the language really used by men. The grandeur of *Paradise Lost* or *Samson Agonistes* could never, by any conceivable device of chemistry or magic, be compounded from delicate sensibilities and a superfine ear for music. For the material of those palaces whole provinces were pillaged, and the waste might furnish forth a city.

CHAPTER III

A PREROGATIVE place among the great epics of the world has sometimes been claimed for *Paradise Lost*, on the ground that the theme it handles is vaster and of a more universal human interest than any handled by Milton's predecessors. It concerns itself with the fortunes, not of a city or an empire, but of the whole human race, and with that particular event in the history of the race which has moulded all its destinies. Around this event, the plucking of an apple, are ranged, according to the strictest rules of the ancient epic, the histories of Heaven and Earth and Hell. The scene of the action is Universal Space. The time represented is Eternity. The characters are God and all his Creatures. And all these are exhibited in the clearest and most inevitable relation with the main event, so that there is not an incident, hardly a line of the poem, but leads backwards or forwards to those central lines in the Ninth Book :—

> So saying, her rash hand in evil hour
> Forth-reaching to the fruit, she plucked, she eat.
> Earth felt the wound, and Nature from her seat,
> Sighing through all her works, gave signs of woe
> That all was lost.

From this point radiates a plot so immense in scope, that the history of the world from the first preaching of the Gospel to the Millennium occupies only some fifty lines of Milton's epilogue. And if the plot be vast, the stage is large enough to set it forth. The size of Milton's theatre gives to his imagination those colossal scenical opportunities which are turned to such magnificent account. De Quincey enumerates some of them—" Heaven opening to eject her rebellious children ; the un-voyageable depths of ancient Chaos, with its 'anarch old' and its eternal war of wrecks ; these traversed by that great leading Angel that drew after him the third part of the heavenly host ; earliest Paradise dawning upon the warrior-angel out of this far-distant 'sea without shore' of chaos ; the dreadful phantoms of Sin and Death, prompted by secret sympathy and snuffing the distant scent of 'mortal change on earth,' chasing the steps of their great progenitor and sultan ; finally the heart-freezing visions, shown and nar-rated to Adam, of human misery through vast successions of shadowy generations : all these scenical opportunities offered in the *Paradise Lost* become in the hands of the mighty artist elements of undying grandeur not matched on earth."

All these grandeurs and beauties are as real and living to-day as they were on the day when Milton conceived them. But the other advantage claimed for his epic, that it deals with matters of the dearest concern to all of us, has been sharply questioned. It was Mr. Pattison's complaint of *Paradise Lost* that in it "Milton has taken a scheme of life for life itself," and that it requires a violent effort from the modern reader to accommodate his conceptions to the anthropomorphic theology of the poem. The world is now thickly peopled with men and women who, having bestowed their patronage on other ancestors, care little about Adam and Eve, and who therefore feel that Milton's poem is wanting in the note of actuality. Satan himself is not what he used to be ; he is doubly fallen, in the esteem of his victims as well as of his Maker, and indeed

> Comes to the place where he before had sat
> Among the prime in splendour, now deposed,
> Ejected, emptied, gazed, unpitied, shunned,
> A spectacle of ruin.

" He who aspires," says Mr. Pattison, " to be the poet of a nation is bound to adopt a hero who is already dear to that people." But how if the hero subsequently fall out of vogue, and his name

lose its power with a fickle populace? Can even
a poet save him?

The drifting away of the popular belief from
the tenets of Milton's theology doubtless does
something to explain the lukewarm interest taken
by most educated English readers in *Paradise
Lost*. But it is a mistake to make much of this
explanation. Certainly Milton held his own
theological beliefs, as expounded in the poem, in
perfect good faith and with great tenacity. But
the generation after his own, which first gave him
his great fame, was not seduced into admiration
by any whole-hearted fellowship in belief. Dryden
laments the presence in the poem of so many
" machining persons,"—as he calls the supernatural
characters of *Paradise Lost*. At almost the same
date Dr. Thomas Burnet was causing a mild sen-
sation in the theological world by expounding the
earlier chapters of the Book of Genesis in an
allegorical sense, and denying to them the signifi-
cance of a literal history. Voltaire, while he praises
Milton, remarks that the topic of *Paradise Lost*
has afforded nothing among the French but some
lively lampoons, and that those who have the
highest respect for the mysteries of the Christian
religion cannot forbear now and then making free
with the devil, the serpent, the frailty of our first
parents, and the rib that was stolen from Adam.
" I have often admired," he goes on, "how barren

the subject appears, and how fruitful it grows under his hands."

It seems likely that Milton himself, before he was fairly caught in the mesh of his own imagination, was well aware that his subject demanded something of the nature of a *tour de force*. He had to give physical, geometric embodiment to a far-reaching scheme of abstract speculation and thought,—parts of it very reluctant to such a treatment. The necessities of the epic form constrained him. When Satan, on the top of Mount Niphates, exclaims—

Which way I fly is Hell; myself am Hell;

when Michael promises to Adam, after his expulsion from the garden—

A Paradise within thee; happier far;

Milton must have known as well as any of his critics that this conception of Hell and of Paradise, if insisted on, would have shattered the fabric of his poem. His figures of Sin and Death were of his own invention, and we must not suppose him so obtuse as never to have realised the part that his shaping imagination bore in the presentment of other and greater figures in the poem. In some respects he tried rather to impose a scheme of thought and imagination upon his age than to express the ideas that he found current. His theology and his cosmical conceptions are equally tainted with his individual heresies. He flies in the face of the Athanasian Creed by representing the generation of the Son as an event occurring in time—" on such day as Heaven's great year brings forth." His later poem of *Paradise Regained* and the posthumous treatise of Christian Doctrine show him an Arian ; in the poem the Almighty is made to speak of

> This perfect man, by merit called my Son.

His account of the creation of the World as a mere ordering or re-arrangement of the wild welter of an uncreated material Chaos receives no countenance from the Fathers. In many points of theological teaching he is compelled to form definite and even visual conceptions where orthodoxy had cautiously confined itself to vague general propositions. So that the description of Sin and Death and of the causeway built by them between Hellgates and the World, much as it has been objected to even by admirers of the poem, is only an extreme instance of the defining and hardening process that Milton found needful throughout for the concrete presentment of the high doings which are his theme. He congealed the mysteries of Time and Space, Love and Death, Sin and Forgiveness, into a material system ; and in so doing, while paying the utmost deference to his authorities, he yet exercised many a choice with regard

to matters indifferent or undefinable. Thus, for
instance, he borrows from the Talmud the notion
that Satan first learned the existence of a prohibited
tree from overhearing a conversation between
Adam and Eve. He was surely conscious of what
he was doing, and would have been not ill-pleased
to learn that the Universe, as he conceived of it,
has since been called by his name. It is Milton's
Paradise Lost, lost by Milton's Adam and Eve,
who are tempted by Milton's Satan, and punished
by Milton's God. The stamp of his clear hard
imagination is on the whole fabric ; and it is not
much harder for us to coax ourselves into the
belief that his is indeed the very world we inhabit
than it was for the men of his own time. The
senses and the intellect are older than modern
science, and were employed to good effect before
the invention of the spectroscope ; it is they in
their daily operation that make it difficult to leap
the gulf which separates the amenities and trivi-
alities of common life from the solemn theatre
of the poet's imagination. The objection that the
poem has lost much of its value because we are
compelled to imagine where our elders believed is
of little weight in a case like this, where our lack
of belief is not brought home to us until insuper-
able difficulties are placed in the way of our
imagination. Where Milton was freest, there we
follow him most gladly ; where he wrote in fetters,

as notably in some of the scenes transacted in Heaven, our imagination, not our belief, is the first to rebel.

We are deceived by names ; the more closely *Paradise Lost* is studied, the more does the hand of the author appear in every part. The epic poem, which in its natural form is a kind of cathedral for the ideas of a nation, is by him transformed into a chapel-of-ease for his own mind, a monument to his own genius and his own habits of thought. The *Paradise Lost* is like the sculptured tombs of the Medici in Florence ; it is not of Night and Morning, nor of Lorenzo and Giovanni, that we think as we look at them, but solely of the great creator, Michael Angelo. The same dull convention that calls the *Paradise Lost* a religious poem might call these Christian statues. Each is primarily a great work of art ; in each the traditions of two eras are blended in a unity that is indicative of nothing but the character and powers of the artist. The *Paradise Lost* is not the less an eternal monument because it is a monument to dead ideas.

We do not know exactly when Milton made his choice of subject. His Latin verses addressed to Manso, Marquis of Villa, in January 1638-9, show that Arthur and the Round Table was at that time the uppermost theme in his mind, and that the warlike achievement of heroes was the aspect of it that most attracted him. After his return to England in 1639, it is mentioned once again in his elegy on Charles Diodati, and then we hear no more of it. In the tentative list of subjects, made in 1641, Arthur has disappeared, and the story of *Paradise Lost* already occupies the most conspicuous place, with four separate drafts suggesting different treatments of the theme.

It would be idle to speculate on what Milton might have made of the Arthur legends. One thing is certain; he would have set up the warrior king as a perfectly objective figure, hampered by no allegory, and with no inward and spiritual signification. The national cause, maintained heroically in a hundred battles, and overwhelmed at last by the brute violence of the foreign oppressor, was subject enough for him; he would never have marred his epic by sickly irresolution and the struggles of a divided will in the principal characters. Perhaps his mind reverted to his old dreams when he came to describe the pastimes wherewith the rebel angels beguile their time in Hell :—

> Others, more mild,
> Retreated in a silent valley, sing
> With notes angelical to many a harp
> Their own heroic deeds, and hapless fall
> By doom of battle, and complain that Fate
> Free Virtue should enthrall to Force or Chance.
> Their song was partial ; but the harmony

> (What could it less when Spirits immortal sing ?)
> Suspended Hell, and took with ravishment
> The thronging audience.

This is only one of the very numerous places in *Paradise Lost* where, before he is well aware of it, we catch Milton's sympathies dilating themselves upon the wrong side.

His researches in British annals, begun at the time when he was still in quest of a theme, convinced him that the whole story of Arthur was "obscured and blemished with fables." He foraged among other British subjects, feeling that the great poem which was designed to raise England to the literary peerage and set her by the side of countries of older fame must deal with a theme of truly national import. Some of the subjects that he jotted down were obviously of too incidental and trivial a nature for his purpose, and a wise instinct confined him to the earlier history of the island, where his own freedom of treatment was less likely to be hampered by an excess of detail. And then, precisely how or when we do not know, the idea came to him that he would treat a subject still larger and of a more tremendous import,— the fortunes, not of the nation, but of the race :—

> With loss of Eden, till one greater Man
> Restore us, and regain the blissful seat.

The attractions that this theme, once hit on,

exercised on Milton's mind may easily be guessed. In the first place, it was a sacred subject : an opportunity for leading poetry back to its divine allegiance; and, by the creation of a new species of epic, an escape from a danger which must have been very present to his mind—the danger of too close an imitation of the ancients. More specific reasons concurred in recommending it. In the Garden of Eden he might present to an age which was overrun with a corrupt religion and governed by a decadent court the picture of a religion without a church, of life in its primitive simplicity, and of patriarchal worship without the noisome accretions of later ceremonial. His attitude to the Laudian movement is eloquently expressed, at this same time, in the treatise *Of Reformation in England*, where he describes how the religious teachers of his own and preceding ages "began to draw down all the divine intercourse betwixt God and the soul, yea, the very shape of God himself into an exterior and bodily form, urgently pretending a necessity and obligement of joining the body in a formal reverence and worship circumscribed; they hallowed it, they fumed it, they sprinkled it, they bedecked it, not in robes of pure innocency, but of pure linen, with other deformed and fantastic dresses, in palls and mitres, gold, and gewgaws fetched from Aaron's old wardrobe or the flamen's vestry : then was the priest set to con his motions and his postures, his liturgies and his lurries, till the soul by this means of over-bodying herself, given up justly to fleshly delights, bated her wing apace downward : and finding the ease she had from her visible and sensuous colleague, the body, in performance of religious duties, her pinions now broken and flagging, shifted off from herself the labour of high soaring any more, forgot her heavenly flight, and left the dull and droiling carcase to plod on in the old road and drudging trade of outward conformity."

But Adam and Eve, Milton is careful to explain, were not ritualists. They recite their evening hymn of praise as they stand at the entrance to their shady lodge : —

> This said unanimous, and other rites
> Observing none, but adoration pure
> Which God likes best, into their inmost bower
> Handed they went.

The traits of Milton's Puritanism peep out at unexpected places in the poem. The happy Garden, Adam is told, will be destroyed after the Flood, for a reason that would have been approved by the image-breakers of the Commonwealth : —

> To teach thee that God attributes to place
> No sanctity, if none be thither brought
> By men who there frequent, or therein dwell.

The palace of Pandemonium is built by Satan's host in an hour, whence men may

> Learn how their greatest monuments of fame,
> And strength, and art, are easily outdone
> By spirits reprobate ;

—a perfectly sound moral, well illustrating Mr. Swinburne's remark that Puritanism has nothing to do with Art, and that the great Puritans and the great artists have never confused them.

Milton must also have been drawn to the theme of *Paradise Lost* by the scope it promised for scenes of quiet natural beauty :—

> All that bowery loneliness,
> The brooks of Eden mazily murmuring
> And bloom profuse and cedar arches.

His imagination was so susceptible to a touch of beauty that even in the bare sketch he has left for a drama dealing with the story of Lot and his escape from Sodom we see how likely he was, here also, to fall into the error of *Comus*. As Lot entertains the angels at supper, " the Gallantry of the town passe by in Procession, with musick and song, to the temple of Venus Urania." The opening Chorus is to relate the course of the city, " each evening every one with mistresse, or Ganymed, gitterning along the streets, or solacing on the banks of Jordan, or down the stream." But in the story of the Garden of Eden the beauty was, for once, on the side of the morality; innocence and purity might be depicted, not, as in a fallen world, clad in complete steel, but at ease in their native haunts, surrounded by all the inexhaustible bounty of an unsubdued and uncorrupted Nature.

The chief dramatic interest of the poem, however, comes in with the great outcast angel, stirred up by his passions of envy and revenge to assault the new-created inhabitants of the Garden. It seems likely that Milton was drawn to this part of his theme by chains of interest and sympathy stronger than he confessed or knew. He was an epic poet, striving to describe great events worthily, but the dramatic situation betrayed him. He knew only that he could draw a rebel leader, noble in bearing, superbly outlined, a worthy adversary of the Most High. But it happened to him, as it has happened to others who have found themselves in a position where Satan could do them a service; before long, as if by some mediæval compact, the relations are reversed, and the poet is in the service of the Devil. He can hardly have foreseen this chance; although there are not wanting signs in the poem itself that, before it was half completed, he became uneasily conscious of what was happening, and attempted, too late, to remedy it. When he chose his subject he doubtless intended that the centre of interest should be fixed in the Garden of Eden, and did not perceive how of necessity it must tend to sink lower, to that realm in the shadow of darkness, innumerably more populous, inhabited by beings of a nobler origin, of greater (and more human) passions, with a longer and more distinguished history, and with this further claim upon the sympathy of the reader, that they are doomed to an eternity of suffering.

It is worth our while as critics to try to put ourselves in Milton's place at the time when he had made his choice, that we may realise not only the attractions but also the difficulties of the theme. An Italian poet of the early seventeenth century, Giovanni Battista Andreini, from whose drama, entitled *Adamo*, Milton is alleged to have borrowed some trifles, has made a very full and satisfactory statement of these difficulties in the preface to his play.   He mentions, for instance, the unpromising monotony of Adam's life during the time spent in the earthly paradise, and the difficulty of giving verisimilitude to the conversation between the woman and the snake.   But he waxes most eloquent on the last and greatest difficulty — " since the composition must remain deprived of those poetic ornaments so dear to the Muses ; deprived of the power to draw comparisons from implements of art introduced in the course of years, since in the time of the first man there was no such thing ; deprived also of naming (at least while Adam speaks or discourse is held with him), for example, bows, arrows, hatchets, urns, knives, swords, spears, trumpets, drums, trophies, banners, lists, hammers, torches, bellows, funeral piles, theatres, exchequers, infinite things of a like nature, introduced by the necessities of sin ; . . . deprived moreover of introducing points of history, sacred or profane, of relating fictions of fabulous deities, of rehearsing loves, furies, sports of hunting or fishing, triumphs, shipwrecks, conflagrations, enchantments, and things of a like nature, that are in truth the ornament and the soul of poetry."

All these difficulties for Andreini's drama were difficulties also for Milton's poem. Yet no reader of *Paradise Lost* is found to complain that the poem is lacking in poetic ornament. Milton has successfully surmounted or evaded many of this formidable catalogue of limitations, without the sacrifice of dramatic propriety. It is true that in the course of their morning orisons, addressed to their Maker, Adam and Eve apostrophise the Mists and Exhalations—

> that now rise
> From hill or steaming lake, dusky or gray,
> Till the sun paint your fleecy skirts with gold ;

—where, a purist might urge, neither of them had any right to be acquainted with paint, or skirts, or gold. But anachronisms like these are, after all, only a part of the great anachronism, or postulate rather, whereby Adam and Eve are made to speak the English tongue. In the Twelfth Book Michael is guilty of a graver lapse where he mentions baptism without explanation or apology. On the other hand, Raphael, who had a pleasanter occasion and more time for his retrospective summary, explains the military manœuvring of angels by what Adam had already seen of the flight of birds, and after describing the great war in Heaven and the fierce hosting of the opposed forces, ventures, at a later point in his story, to illustrate the flowing together of the congregated waters at the Creation by a simile drawn, with apology, from the massing of troops :—

> As armies at the call
> Of trumpet (for of armies thou hast heard)
> Troop to their standard, so the watery throng,
> Wave rolling after wave.

In the main Milton studies propriety with regard to the forbidden matters enumerated by Andreini. But he escapes from the full effect of the prohibition by a variety of devices. In the first place, there are the two chief episodes of the poem ; Raphael's narration, from the Fifth to the Eighth Book, imparted to Adam as a warning against impending dangers, and conveying an account of the history of the Universe before the Creation of Man ; and Michael's narration, in the Eleventh and Twelfth Books, consoling and strengthening Adam, before the Expulsion from the Garden, by a rapid survey of the prospective history of the World from that event down to the Millennium. Considered as a narrator, Michael is very subject to dullness; were it not for the unfailing dignity and magniloquence of his diction, his tale would be merely a bleak compendium of the outlines of Scripture history; but to Raphael is committed the story of the war in Heaven and its amazing sequel,—a story containing passages so brilliant, and so little necessary to be narrated at length, that there is some flavour of inconsistency in Milton's apology for his theme, prefixed to the Ninth Book, where he describes himself as—

> Not sedulous by nature to indite
> Wars, hitherto the only argument
> Heroic deemed, chief mastery to dissect
> With long and tedious havoc fabled knights
> In battles feigned (the better fortitude
> Of patience and heroic martyrdom
> Unsung), or to describe races and games
> Or tilting furniture, emblazoned shields,
> Impresses quaint, caparisons and steeds,
> Bases and tinsel trappings, gorgeous knights
> At joust and tournament; then marshalled feast
> Served up in hall with sewers and seneschals:
> The skill of artifice and office mean;
> Not that which justly gives heroic name
> To person or to poem! Me, of these
> Nor skilled nor studious, higher argument
> Remains, sufficient of itself to raise
> That name, unless an age too late, or cold
> Climate, or years, damp my intended wing

> Depressed ; and much they may if all be mine,
> Not hers who brings it nightly to my ear.

To depreciate war as a subject for the heroic
Muse was ungrateful in Milton, who had devoted
the whole of his Sixth Book to a description
of the " wild work in Heaven" caused by the
great rebellion, and had indulged his imagination
with some most extravagant fantasies ; such as
the digging in the soil of Heaven for sulphur
and nitre (where the soil of Hell, it may be
remarked, yielded gold to the miner), the invention of artillery, and the use of mountains
as missiles,

> Hurled to and fro with jaculation dire.

He had, moreover, attained to the height of the
sublime in that terrific closing scene where the Son,
riding forth in single majesty, drives the rebel host
over the crystal bounds of Heaven into the wasteful abyss.   Wars, in short, hold a conspicuous
place in the poem, — conflicts and broils so
enormous that—

> War seemed a civil game {
> To this uproar.

Races and athletic sports are among the melancholy diversions of the dwellers in Hell during
their forced leisure.   Even tilts and tournaments
are not absent from *Paradise Lost*, but they are

introduced by the second of the devices which enable Milton to extend the scope of his poem ; the free and frequent use, namely, of illustrative and decorative comparisons. Thus the spacious hall of Pandemonium is compared to—

> A covered field, where champions bold
> Wont ride in armed, and at the Soldan's chair
> Defied the best of Panim chivalry
> To mortal combat, or career with lance.

It is plain that although almost all of the characters of the poem are precluded from making allusion to the events of human history, the poet himself is free ; and he uses his freedom throughout. Most of the passages that have gained for Milton the name of a learned poet are introduced by way of simile. At times he employs the simplest epic figure, drawn from the habits of rustic or animal life. But his favourite figure is the " long-tailed simile," or, as it is better called, the decorative comparison, used for its ennobling, rather than for its elucidating virtue. Here he parts company with Homer, and even with Virgil, who could draw on no such vast and various store of history, geography, and romance. From Herodotus to Olaus Magnus, and onward to the latest discoveries in geography and astronomy, the researches of Galileo, and the descriptions given by contemporary travellers of China and the Chinese, or of the

North American Indians, Milton compels the authors he had read, both ancient and modern, to contribute to the gracing of his work. It is partly this wealth of implicit lore, still more, perhaps, the subtly reminiscent character of much of his diction, that justifies Mr. Pattison in the remark that "an appreciation of Milton is the last reward of consummated scholarship."

A third device, not the least remarkable of those by which he gives elasticity to his theme, is to be found in the tradition that he adopts with regard to the later history of the fallen angels. A misunderstanding of four verses in the fourteenth chapter of Isaiah, and some cryptic allusions in the Book of Revelations are the chief Scriptural authorities for the Miltonic account of the Fall of the Angels, which is not borrowed from the Fathers, but corresponds rather with the later version popularised in England by the cycles of Miracle Plays. According to the *Divine Institutes* of Lactantius, the nameless Angel, to whom from the first had been given power over the new-created Earth, was alone infected with envy of the Son of God, his elder and superior, and set himself to vitiate and destroy mankind in the cradle. He tempted Eve, and she fell ; after the expulsion from Paradise he set himself also to corrupt the guardian angels who were sent down from Heaven for the protection and education of the increasing race of men. In this attempt also he succeeded ; "the sons of God saw the daughters of men that they were fair, and they took them wives of all which they chose." And they forgot their heavenly estate, and made for themselves a Godless dominion upon Earth. This is the Fall of the Angels as it is narrated at greater length in the recently recovered apocryphal *Book of Enoch*, and alluded to, perhaps in the Epistles of Peter and of Jude, where are mentioned "the angels that sinned," and "the angels which kept not their first estate." Milton's version brings these angels to the earth, not as protectors of mankind, but as conquerors come from Hell, to possess and occupy the spacious world delivered over to them by the victory of Satan. From that point forward, however, he adopts the tradition whereby Jerome, Lactantius, and others had identified the fallen angels with the gods of the heathen. Whether as conquerors or as corrupted guardians of the human race, they seek the same ends,—to divert worship from the true God, and by the destruction of man, to contrive a solace for their own perdition. They are the inventors of astrology, sooth-saying, divination, necromancy, and black magic ; they were once the ministers of God, and still have a presentiment of his acts, so that they can sometimes speak truly of the future by means of oracles and magicians, claiming the while the credit of bringing that to pass which in fact they only foresaw. Milton, in adopting this doctrine, merely followed current belief, and did not, as De Quincey seems to think, hit upon it by a fortunate stroke of genius. He might have found it incidentally but fully set forth in so recent a book as Hooker's *Ecclesiastical Polity*, I. iv. " The fall of the angels, therefore," says Hooker, "was pride. Since their fall, their practices have been the clean contrary unto those just mentioned. For, being dispersed, some in the air, some in the earth, some in the water, some among the minerals, dens, and caves that are under the earth ; they have by all means laboured to effect a universal rebellion against the laws, and as far as in them lieth utter destruction of the works of God. These wicked spirits the heathen honoured instead of Gods, both generally under the name of *dii inferi*, 'gods infernal,' and particularly, some in oracles, some in idols, some as household gods, some as nymphs ; in a word, no foul or wicked spirit which was not one way or other honoured of men as god, till such time as light appeared in the world, and dissolved the works of the Devil." The argument which Milton himself sets forth for the support of this view was accepted as conclusive in his own age. The Ionian gods, he says, Titan, and Saturn, and Jove, and the rest, the youngest branch of that evil and influential family, were—

Held
Gods, yet confessed later than Heaven and Earth
Their boasted parents.

They ruled the middle air and had access to no
higher or purer heaven. Howsoever Milton came
by the doctrine, it was of enormous use to him ;
it gave him names for his devils, and characters,
and a detailed history of the part they had played
in human affairs ; it was, in short, a key to all the
mythologies.

By these devices the author of *Paradise Lost*
escapes the impoverishment of imagination that
his subject seemed to impose upon him. On
looking once more over Andreini's list of prohibited topics, we are surprised to find how many
of them Milton has found a place for. He does
introduce points of history, sacred and profane ;
he relates fictions of fabulous deities ; he rehearses
loves, furies, triumphs, conflagrations, and things
of a like nature. The principal conflagration that
he describes is on a very large scale ; and the
majestic ascent of the Son—

Up to the Heaven of Heavens, his high abode,
.   .   .   .   .   .

Followed with acclamation, and the sound
Symphonious of ten thousand harps, that tuned
Angelic harmonies,

is the grandest triumphal procession in all literature.
On the other hand, he manages to dispense with

some of the institutions and implements "introduced by the necessities of sin." He has swords and spears, trumpets and drums in plenty. But he has no knives, nor hatchets, nor bellows ; and no theatres nor exchequers. There are no urns nor funeral piles, because there is no death ; or rather, because the only Death that there is increases the number of persons in the poem by one. Sports of hunting and fishing there are, of course, none ; and, although it is an heroic poem, the horse takes little part in the celestial war, is hardly known in hell, and is unheard of on earth until Adam beholds in vision the armed concourse of his corrupt descendants. Nevertheless, the general impression left by the poem is one of richness rather than poverty of poetic ornament. The wealth is most profusely displayed in the books treating of Satan and his followers, but it is not absent from Eden nor from the empyreal Heaven, although in the one case the monotony of the situation, and in the other the poet's evident anxiety to authorise his every step from Scripture, prevent the full display of his power. But Milton is a difficult poet to disable ; he is often seen at his best on the tritest theme, which he handles after his own grave fashion by comprehensive statement, measured and appropriate, heightened by none save the most obvious metaphors, and depending for almost all its charm on the quiet colouring of the inevitable epithet, and the solemn music of the cadence :—

> Now came still Evening on, and Twilight gray
> Had in her sober livery all things clad ;
> Silence accompanied ; for beast and bird
> They to their grassy couch, these to their nests,
> Were slunk, all but the wakeful nightingale.
> She all night long her amorous descant sung :
> Silence was pleased.   Now glowed the firmament
> With living sapphires ; Hesperus, that led
> The starry host, rode brightest, till the Moon,
> Rising in clouded majesty, at length
> Apparent queen, unveiled her peerless light,
> And o'er the dark her silver mantle threw.

Darkness, silence, rest, the nightingale's song, the stars, the rising of the moon—these are all the material of this wonderful passage.   Yet did ever such beauty fall with night upon such peace, save in Paradise alone ?

Once he had got his story, based on his few authorities, with hints unconsciously taken and touches added, perhaps, from his reading of other poets—of Cædmon, Andreini, and Vondel, of Spenser, Sylvester, Crashaw, and the Fletchers— Milton's first task was to reduce it to the strict relations of time and space.   His blindness probably helped him by relieving him from the hourly solicitations of the visible world, and giving him a dark and vacant space in which to rear his geometric fabric.   Against this background the figures of his characters are outlined in shapes of light, and in this vacancy he mapped out his local Heaven and Hell.

Heaven, as Milton portrays it, is a plain of vast extent, diversified with hills, valleys, woods and streams. In the Second Book he speaks of it as—

> Extended wide
> In circuit, undetermined square or round ;

in the Tenth Book it is determined, and is square. It is bounded by battlements of living sapphire, and towers of opal. In the midst is situated a Mount, the dwelling place of the Most High, surrounded by golden lamps, which diffuse night and day alternately—for without twilight and dawn, his dearest memories, Heaven would have been no Heaven to Milton. On a mountain far to the north of this great plain, Satan erects his pyramids and towers of diamond and gold, and establishes his empire, which lasts exactly three days. At his final overthrow the crystal wall of Heaven rolls back, disclosing a gap into the abyss ; the rebels, tortured with plagues and thunder, fling themselves in desperation over the verge. They fall for nine days, through Chaos. Chaos is the realm of a king of the same name, who reigns over it with his consort Night. It is of immeasurable extent, quite dark, and turbulent with the raw material of the Cosmos. Just as Milton, for the purposes of his poem, adopted the older astronomy, and gave to it a new lease of life in the popular imagination, so also he abides by the older physics. The orderly created World, or Cosmos, is conceived as compounded of four elements, Earth, Air, Fire, and Water. None of these four is to be found in Chaos, for each of them is composed of the simpler atoms of Hot, Cold, Moist, and Dry, symmetrically arranged in pairs. Thus Air is Hot and Moist, Fire is Hot and Dry, Water is Cold and Moist, Earth is Cold and Dry. Before they are separated and blended by Divine command, the four rudimentary constituents of creation are crowded in repulsive contiguity; they bubble and welter, fight and jostle in the dark, with hideous noises. In its upper strata Chaos is calmer, and is faintly lighted by the effulgence from the partially transparent walls of Heaven.

Below is Hell, newly prepared for the rebels. Like Heaven it is a vast plain; a bituminous lake, played over by livid flames, is one of its principal features; and hard by stands a volcanic mountain, at the foot of which the devils build their palace, and hold their assembly. The nine-fold gates of Hell, far distant, are guarded by Sin and Death, the paramour and the son of Satan. No one has plausibly explained how they came by their office. It was intended to be a perfect sinecure; there was no one to be let in and no one to be let out. The single occasion that presented itself for a neglect of their duty was by them eagerly seized.

During the nine days while the rebels lay on the burning lake, drowsed by its fumes, the World was created. It consists, according to the astronomy followed by Milton, of ten concentric spheres fitted, like Chinese boxes, one within another, and the Earth in the centre. Nine of these are transparent, the spheres, that is to say, of the seven planets (the Sun and the Moon being reckoned as planets), the sphere of the fixed stars, and the crystalline sphere. The outermost sphere, or *primum mobile*, is opaque and impervious. The whole orbicular World hangs by a golden chain from that part of the battlements of Heaven whence the angels fell. It is connected with Heaven by richly jewelled stairs, to be let down or taken up at pleasure, and can be entered only through an orifice or passage at the top. Between the foot of the stairs and the entrance to the World is a sea or lake of jasper and liquid pearl.

All the interest and meaning of the World is centred in one favoured spot of Earth. Eden is a district of Mesopotamia, and the happy garden, called Paradise, is situated in the east of Eden. It is a raised table-land, surrounded on all sides by a high ridge of hill, thickly wooded, and impenetrable. Its single gate, hewn out of a rock of alabaster, faces eastward, and is accessible only by a pass leading up from the plain and overhung by craggy cliffs. Through Eden runs a river which passes by a tunnel under Paradise, and, rising through the porous earth, waters the garden with springs. It was by this underground passage that Satan entered the garden a second time, when, having been discovered by Ithuriel, and expelled by Gabriel, he had circled the Earth seven times, keeping on the shady side to avoid the gaze of Uriel, and at the end of the week had resolved on another attempt.

The Fall of Man wrought some few changes in the physical configuration of the Universe. Sin and Death built the mighty causeway that connects the orifice of the World with Hell-gates. Provision had to be made under the new dispensation for the peopling of the whole surface of the Earth ; so the axis was turned askew, and the beginning ordained of extremes of cold and heat, of storms and droughts, and noxious planetary influences. Night and day were known to man in his sinless state, but the seasons date from his transgression.

The time-scheme of the poem is less carefully defined; indeed, it is not certain that Milton intended accurately to define it. The recurrence of the numbers three and nine, numbers traditionally honoured by poetry, throws suspicion on the efforts of the exact commentators. Even in his statements with regard to spatial relations the poet was not always minutely consistent with himself. The distance from the plain of Heaven to the plain of Hell is said in the First Book to be three times the radius of the World, or, in his own words, the prison of Hell is

> As far removed from God and light of Heaven
> As from the centre thrice to the utmost pole.

The great globe, therefore, that hangs from the floor of Heaven reaches two-thirds of the way down to Hell. Yet in the Second Book Satan, after a long and perilous journey from Hell, comes in view of

> This pendent World, in bigness as a star
> Of smallest magnitude close by the moon.

So small is the World, compared with the wide extent of the empyreal Heaven. But it is not easy to conceive how, in the limited space between Heaven and Hell, the World could so appear to Satan.

A like curious consideration of the passages where time is mentioned reveals a gap in the tale of days enumerated by Milton. We are not told how long it took Satan to reach the Earth. Driven back on precedents and analogies we find them conflicting. The outcast angels took nine days to fall the same distance. But falling, as Moloch points out in his speech at the Infernal Council, was to them less natural than rising ; and Raphael,

who was subsequently sent to guard the gates of
Hell during the Creation, made the ascent easily
in part of a day. If we allow a day and a night
for Satan's exploratory voyage, the action of the
poem, from the heavenly decree which occasioned
the rebellion, to the expulsion of Adam and Eve
from Paradise, has been found to occupy thirty-
three days, some measured by a heavenly, some by
an earthly standard. This would make Adam and
Eve about ten days old when they fell. But St.
Augustine says that they spent six years in the
Earthly Paradise, and the question is better left
open.

A graver inconsistency is brought to light by
a close study of the framework of the poem.
Milton seems to have hesitated as to which of two
theories he would adopt concerning the Creation
of Man. After their fall both Satan and Beelzebub
mention a rumour which had long been current
in Heaven of a new race, called Man, shortly
to be created. That rumour could hardly have
reached the rebels during the progress of the
war. Yet in the Seventh Book the Creation
appears as a compliment paid to Satan, a counter-
move devised after the suppression of the great
rebellion. The Omnipotent thus declares his
intention :—

> But, lest his heart exalt him in the harm
> Already done, to have dispeopled Heaven—

> My damage fondly deemed,—I can repair
> That detriment, if such it be to lose
> Self-lost, and in a moment will create
> Another world ; out of one man a race
> Of men innumerable.

This last is the account we must accept. Milton no doubt was attracted by the dramatic superiority of this version, which makes the Creation of Man a minor incident in the great war, so that the human race comes, a mere token and pawn—

> Between the pass and fell incensed points
> Of mighty opposites.

But he was probably also aware that this view had not the highest warrant of orthodoxy.

There is something absurd, perhaps even something repulsive, to the modern mind in this careful, matter-of-fact anatomy of Milton's poem. But it is a useful and necessary exercise, for all his greatest effects are achieved in the realm of the physical and moral sublime, where the moral relations are conditioned chiefly by the physical. There is no metaphysic, nothing spiritual, nothing mysterious, except in name, throughout the whole poem. The so-called spiritual beings are as definitely embodied as man. The rules that Milton followed in dealing with his heavenly essences are very fully laid down in the *Treatise of Christian Doctrine*. He consigned the Fathers

I

to limbo, and built up his entire system from the words of Scripture. Now the Scriptures, in a hundred passages, attribute human passions and actions to Divine beings. We have no choice, said Milton, but to accept these expressions as the truest to which we can attain. " If after the work of six days it be said of God that 'He rested and was refreshed,' *Exodus*, xxxi. 17 ; if it be said that ' He feared the wrath of the enemy,' *Deuteronomy*, xxxii. 27 ; let us believe that it is not beneath the dignity of God . . . to be refreshed in that which refresheth Him, or to fear in that He feareth." Milton had here the sharp logical dilemma which he loved. Either these expressions are literally true, or they are not. If they are, well and good ; if they are not, how can we hope to frame for ourselves better and truer notions of the Deity than those which he has dictated to us as within the reach of our understanding, and fit and proper for us to entertain ? So also with angelic beings : Milton dismisses the nine orders of the apocryphal hierarchy—although he enumerates five of them, in the wrong order, in the roll of that recurring verse—

Thrones, Dominations, Princedoms, Virtues, Powers—

and bases himself upon Scripture. There he finds mention of seven chief angels, with some kind of pre-eminence enjoyed by Michael. In the poem he finds employment for only four, Michael, Gabriel, Raphael, and Uriel, with a few Seraphim and Cherubim, to whom he invariably, and very improperly, assigns a subordinate position.

His angels fight and play games, as they were doing at the gate of Paradise on the evening when Satan first appeared there. They wear solid armour, and so fall a ready prey to the artillery of their foes—

> Unarmed they might
> Have easily, as spirits, evaded swift
> By quick contraction or remove ; but now
> Foul dissipation followed, and forced rout.

They eat and drink and digest ; they even—and here, though we be armed with triple brass, we cannot avoid a sense of shock—they even blush when an indiscreet question is asked of them. When Raphael colours at the inquisitive demands of Adam, it gives a melancholy force to his earlier suggestion—

> What if Earth
> Be but the shadow of Heaven, and things therein
> Each to other like more than on Earth is thought ?

This is the scheme of things, and these are the actors, that Milton sets in motion. We shall do well to accept the limitations he assigns, and to look in his poem only for what is to be found there. It would be a wearisome and fruitless quest to journey through the *Paradise Lost* in search of those profound touches of humanity, and those sudden felicities of insight, which abound in the Elizabethans. Subtleties of thought, fine observation of truths that almost evade the attempt to express them, sentences and figures illuminative of the mysteries of human destiny and the intricacies of human character—of all these there is none. If an author's works are to be used as a treasury or garner of wise and striking sayings, the harvest of sensibility and experience, *Paradise Lost* will yield only a poor handful of gleanings. One such reflection, enforced by a happy figure, occurs in the Third Book, where Satan, disguised as a youthful Cherub, deceives the Archangel Uriel—

> So spake the false dissembler unperceived ;
> For neither man nor angel can discern
> Hypocrisy—the only evil that walks
> Invisible, except to God alone,
> By His permissive will, through Heaven and Earth ;
> And oft, though Wisdom wake, Suspicion sleeps
> At Wisdom's gate, and to Simplicity
> Resigns her charge, while Goodness thinks no ill
> Where no ill seems.

Milton plainly had known hypocrisy, and had been deceived by it. But it would be difficult to match this reflection with any single other passage in the whole poem. To say that such reflections are common in Shakespeare would be too moderate a statement ; they are the very air he breathes.

And even in the lesser dramatists the happy embodiment of observation in a telling figure is to be found on every page. An acute criticism, for instance, is condensed in a dramatic form by Ford, where he describes what may be called low politeness—

> Smooth formality
> Is usher to the rankness of the blood,
> But impudence bears up the train.

The peculiar combination of formality and impudence that marks ill-breeding was never more happily described than in this figure ; the mock solemnity of the usher comes first, and is soon followed by the grimacing antics of the page, while each in his own way implies that the advances of courtesy are a pomp and a deceit. Metaphors of the same kind abound in the work of more modern analytic poets. Here is another parable of a door-keeper, more poetic than Milton's :—

> They say that Pity in Love's service dwells,
> A porter at the rosy temple's gate.
> I missed him going ; but it is my fate
> To come upon him now beside his wells ;
> Whereby I know that I Love's temple leave,
> And that the purple doors have closed behind.

In Milton's poetry we find ourselves in a remote atmosphere ; far indeed from the shrewd observation of daily life, farther even from that wonderful analysis of emotion which is the pastime

of Shakespeare and of Meredith. Beautiful
figured writing and keen psychological observation
of this kind are beside the purpose of Milton, and
beyond his power.

For the time we must forego the attempt to
see into the life of things, and must accept in
imagination our position as citizens in this strange
majestic commonwealth of angels and men. It is
no mean city. Noble shapes pass before our eyes.
High language is held, and great wars are waged.
Events of tremendous import roll on to their
destined accomplishment. Golden processions
move across the dim expanse of Chaos. Worlds
are blown and broken like bubbles. There is
concerted song, feasting, and gratulation ; dire
plots are hatched and blaze forth into light ; will
clashes with will ; Heaven opens, and a torrent of
flaming ruin is poured forth into the deep. The
Victor, ensconced in his omnipotence, is fiercely
triumphant ; and in the dark below there is the
dull gleam of unconquered pride, deadly courage,
and immortal despair. But in the midst of all
this vast rivalry of interests and jar of opposed
systems, a cry is heard, like that muffled cry which
caught Macbeth's ear as he nerved himself for his
last fight. It is the cry of the human soul, left
homeless and derelict in a universe where she is the
only alien. For her the amaranth of the empyreal
Heaven is as comfortless as the adamant of Hell.

She has lost her Paradise even while Adam's was building—the Paradise where the flowers fade, and loves and hates are mortal.

In the poem itself signs are not wanting that Milton felt the terrible strain imposed upon him by the intense and prolonged abstraction of his theme—its unreality and superhuman elevation. Some of the comparisons that he chooses to illustrate scenes in Hell are taken from the incidents of simple rustic life, and by their contrast with the lurid creatures of his imagination come like a draught of cold water to a traveller in a tropical waste of sand and thorns. It is almost as if the poet himself were oppressed by the suffocation of the atmosphere that he has created, and, gasping for breath, sought relief by summoning up to remembrance the sweet security of pastoral life. So, when the devils are shrunk to enter Pandemonium, they are compared to

> Faery elves
> Whose midnight revels, by a forest-side
> Or fountain, some belated peasant sees,
> Or dreams he sees, while overhead the Moon
> Sits. arbitress, and nearer to the Earth
> Wheels her pale course.

The rejoicings, again, at the end of the infernal consultation, are described in a figure that makes a like impression, and brings the same momentary relief—

As, when from mountain-tops the dusky clouds
Ascending, while the North-wind sleeps, o'erspread
Heaven's cheerful face, the louring element
Scowls o'er the darkened landskip snow or shower,
If chance the radiant sun, with farewell sweet,
Extend his evening beam, the fields revive,
The birds their notes renew, and bleating herds
Attest their joy, that hill and valley rings.

The splendid artifice of contrast, noted by De Quincey as one of the subtlest of Milton's devices, is illustrated, perhaps, by both these passages. De Quincey instances neither, but chooses, as examples of the way in which two images may act and react, heightening each other by contrast—first, the use of architectural terms in describing Paradise ; next, the exhibition of a banquet in the desert in *Paradise Regained*— "stimulating the sense of its utter solitude and remotion from men and cities" ; and, last and best, the comparison of Satan, in the same poem, to an old man gathering sticks upon a winter's day. "The household image of old age, of human infirmity, and of domestic hearths, are all meant as a machinery for provoking and soliciting the fearful idea to which they are placed in collision, and as so many repelling poles."

This is clever criticism and true philosophy. But the chief effect from the more elaborate figures of this kind is to be found merely in the reprieve and refreshment that they bring. There is a sense of pathos, almost of tears, in being allowed, for one moment only, to taste reality again, to revisit familiar scenes, before we are once more bound on the slow wheel of unnatural events that is urged forward by the poet. Nothing in Eden comes home to the feelings more directly than the simile used to describe Satan as he watches Eve on the morning of the temptation—

> As one who, long in populous city pent,
> Where houses thick and sewers annoy the air,
> Forth issuing on a summer's morn, to breathe
> Among the pleasant villages and farms
> Adjoined, from each thing met conceives delight—
> The smell of grain, or tedded grass, or kine,
> Or dairy, each rural sight, each rural sound—
> If chance with nymph-like step fair virgin pass,
> What pleasing seemed for her now pleases more,
> She most, and in her look sums all delight :
> Such pleasure took the Serpent to behold
> This flowery plot, the sweet recess of Eve.

The Serpent is glad to escape from Hell, to breathe the morning air of Eden. But how glad we are to escape from Eden

> To breathe
> Among the pleasant villages and farms !

There are no villages and farms in Eden, no smell of hay, no sheaves of corn, no cottages, no roads, and no trace of that most human of symbols, the thin blue scarf of smoke rising from a wayside encampment. Even when we are privileged to assist at the first festal celebration of hospitality on Earth, the dinner given to the Angel, for which Eve gathers

> Fruit of all kinds, in coat
> Rough or smooth rined, or bearded husk, or shell,

and heaps them, with bountiful hand, on the table of raised turf, we are not perfectly at ease with our hosts. Not all the dignity of Adam, nor all the beauty of Eve, can make us forget that they are nut-eaters, that they have not the art of cooking, and do not ferment the juice of the grape. A short stay in Eden teaches us the sad truth that we are dependent, not only for the pleasures of our life, but even for many of the dearest pleasures of our imagination, on the devices "introduced by the necessities of sin." We cannot settle down in the midst of this "enormous bliss"; we wander through the place, open-mouthed with wonder, like country visitors admiring the Crown jewels, and then—we long to be at home.

There are no children in any of Milton's poems. The introduction, in *Paradise Lost*, of a real human child, such as Shakespeare brings into *Coriolanus* or *Macbeth*, would be like the bringing of a spark of fire into a powder magazine. None of these edifying speeches could be made in the presence of such an auditor, or such a critic. The whole system would be blown into fragments ; the artificial perspective that Milton preserves with so great care would lose its glamour at a touch. Hell and Heaven and Eden would dissolve away like the baseless fabric of a vision, a scholar's nightmare, if once they were subjected to the free scrutiny of a child.

Paradise Lost will not bear—it could at no time, not even in the most theological of ages, have borne—the more searching tests of realism, of verisimilitude, and credibility. It is all the greater skill in the poet that by his careful handling of our imagination and feelings he actually does produce "that willing suspension of disbelief for the moment which constitutes poetic faith." The less it will endure the trial as a system or theory of the universe, the more wonderful does it appear as a work of art. By the most delicate skill of architecture this gigantic filamented structure has been raised into the air. It looks like some enchanted palace that has lighted on the ground for a moment, resting in its flight. It is really the product of the most elaborate and careful engineering science ; the strains and stresses put on every part of the material have been calculated and allowed for. The poise and balance are so minutely exact that it just stands, and no more. But that it should stand at all is the marvel, seeing that it is spanned on frail arches over the abyss of the impossible, the unnatural, and the grotesque. Let it be granted that, in its main features, the system of *Paradise Lost* does correspond with what was and is the religious creed of not a few people. There is many a religious creed, strongly held, which is convincing enough until the imagination begins to work it out in detail, to try to realise it, in a clear light, as a connected whole. Then either the imagination or the creed must give way. The remarkable thing about Milton's achievement is that *Paradise Lost* is both a creed and a cosmical scheme of imagination, and that, except here and there, it is impossible to point to parts of the poem and say, " Here he ceased to believe," or " Here he gave up the effort to imagine." He both imagined and believed throughout ; he projected himself, like a sleep-walker, into the mammoth caves of his antediluvian dreams, and lived among his own radiant and shadowy creations. We need not, therefore, be surprised to find that, in the first place, his daughters ran wild, and neither liked nor understood their father ; and that, in the second place, for the rendering of his thought he invented a system of preternaturally majestic diction, perfectly fitted for the utterance of his own conceptions, but, when divorced from those conceptions, so monstrously artificial in effect, that his imitators and followers, hoisting themselves on the Miltonic stilts, brought the very name of " poetic diction " into a contempt that has lasted for more than a century, and is not yet wholly extinct.

CHAPTER IV

THE difficulties which Milton felt and conquered
in the making of his epic masterpiece had their
origin, for the most part, in the intractable and
barren nature of his chosen theme. The dangers
that beset him, and sometimes tripped his feet,
arose, on the other hand, from his own declared
intention in the handling of that theme :—

> That, to the highth of this great argument,
> I may assert Eternal Providence
> And justify the ways of God to men.

The pursuit of this argumentative end led him
through strange passes. A less courageous or a
more sensitive man might well have hesitated at
the entrance. But Milton hesitated at nothing.
The ultimate mysteries of human existence and
Divine government were no mysteries to him.

> The living Throne, the sapphire blaze,
> Where angels tremble, while they gaze,
> He saw ;

—and he did not tremble. His persons are visible, their characters are known, the nature of their relations is easily ascertained and expounded. Everything, in short, is as plain as a pikestaff. So he came to picture scenes which criticism is reluctant to traverse, and to make statements which it is equally irreverent either to affirm or to deny.

Dr. Johnson, with a fearful and sincere piety, refused to follow Milton into Heaven. " Of the agents in the poem," he says, " the chief are such as it is irreverence to name on slight occasions." And again :—" The characters in the *Paradise Lost* which admit of examination are those of angels and of man." It is impossible not to respect Johnson's attitude, but later critics have found it difficult to follow his example, and Milton himself would have been the last to claim sanctuary in Heaven for the imaginations on which the whole fabric of the poem depends.

Coleridge is one of the very few critics who have praised the conduct of the celestial part of the story :—" Wherever God is represented as acting directly as Creator, without any exhibition of his own essence, Milton adopts the simplest and sternest language of the Scriptures. . . . But, as some personal interest was demanded for the purposes of poetry, Milton takes advantage of the dramatic representation of God's address to the

Son, the Filial Alterity, and in *those addresses* slips in, as it were by stealth, language of affection, or thought, or sentiment. . . . He was very wise in adopting the strong anthropomorphism of the Hebrew Scriptures at once." Yet this is hardly an answer to the chief objections that have been urged against Milton's conduct of the poem. These are grounded, not on his adoption of the strong anthropomorphism of the Hebrew Scriptures, but on the nature of the matter that he slips in, "as if by stealth," and the character that he attributes to his Divine persons. Had he been a pagan, pure and simple, he might have been frankly and explicitly materialistic in his conceptions. Had he been touched by the spirit of the greatest of Christian poets, he might have shrouded the Godhead in a mystery of silence and light. But he had something to prove to the men of his own time, and neither course served him.

Milton's theodicy is of his own devising, and is neither Catholic nor Calvinist. His heresies may be reduced to a single point; the ultimate basis on which he rests the universe is political, not religious. The fierce simplicity of his processes of thought here led him straight into a trap. Law to him is an expression of Will, enforced by due penalties. As promulgated by human authority, laws are to be obeyed only if they do not clash with the dictates of a higher Power.

The laws of God are subject to no such restraint. They are ; and, save by faith, there is no further word to be said. But Milton had set himself to justify these laws by reason. Destitute as he was of speculative power, he attempted no transcendental amalgam of diverse conceptions, of Love and Law, of Mercy and Justice. He fell back on Law as the naked assertion of Will, and helped out the ancient argument of the pot and the potter with a utilitarian appeal, which he puts into the mouth of a Seraph, to the happy working of the Divine laws in practice.

So it comes about that the main argument of the poem is founded on an outrage done to religion. In the place and under the name of Him " with whom is no variableness, neither shadow of turning," Milton set up in Heaven a whimsical Tyrant, all of whose laws are arbitrary and occasional, and who exacts from his creatures an obedience that differs from brute submission in one point only, that by the gift of free-will it is put within their power to disobey. His commands, like his laws, are issued from time to time. Sometimes they enjoin the impossible on his subjects ; as when Michael and Gabriel, at the head of the heavenly host, are ordered to drive Satan and his crew out of Heaven into the abyss—a task they prove wholly unable to accomplish. Sometimes orders are given merely as an assertion of

K

power, and to test submission ; as when Raphael
is sent to keep the rebels confined in Hell, and
explains subsequently to Adam :—

> Not that they durst without his leave attempt ;
> But us he sends upon his high behests
> For state, as sovran King, and to inure
> Our prompt obedience.

The particular event with which, according to
Milton, the whole history begins is presented with
a crudity that would have horrified the Fathers.
The appointment of a Vicegerent to the Almighty,
and the edict requiring homage to be done to him,
are announced " on a day " to the host of Angels
assembled by special summons for this purpose.
During the night following, one of the chief
Archangels, thereafter called Satan, draws off his
forces to the north under pretext of preparing a
welcome for the new Commander, who is to make
a progress through his domain, promulgating more
new laws. The purpose of the rebels is discerned
by the All-Knowing, who makes this strange
speech to the Son :—

> Let us advise, and to this hazard draw
> With speed what force is left, and all employ
> In our defence, lest unawares we lose
> This our high place, our sanctuary, our hill.

It is unnecessary to quote more of the speeches
in Heaven ; they are tangles of Scriptural phrase,

from which there can be extracted neither good divinity nor good humanity. "The glory of God," says the Wisdom of Solomon, "is to conceal a thing ; the glory of the King is to find it out." But the glory of Milton's Deity is to explain a thing. The proud voluble candour of some of these speeches reminds us only of the author of *A Defence of the People of England.* In some of them there is even a flavour of uneasy boastfulness, as of one who is anxious not to be lessened in the estimation of the rebel adversary.

It may be pleaded that the epical necessities of the poem imposed finite conceptions, of one sort or another, upon Milton; and that, when once he had begun to define and explain, he was carried further and further along that perilous way without being fully conscious of whither he was tending. Yet his persistent accumulation of harsh and dread traits seems wilful in its nature ; he bases his description, no doubt, on hints from Scripture, but he pays no attention to any that do not fall in with his own narrow and gloomy conception. Satan is permitted to rise from the burning lake—

> That with reiterated crimes he might
> Heap on himself damnation.

When he arrives at the foot of the stairway that joins Heaven and the World—

The stairs were then let down, whether to dare
The Fiend by easy ascent, or aggravate
His sad exclusion from the doors of bliss.

Astronomy, it is suggested by " the affable Arch-angel," has perhaps been made a difficult subject in order to produce the droll fallacies of astronomers :

He his fabric of the Heavens
Hath left to their disputes—perhaps to move
His laughter at their quaint opinions wide.

And this conjecture is borne out by what happened when the builders of the tower of Babel were frustrated, for then—

Great laughter was in Heaven,
And looking down to see the hubbub strange
And hear the din.

Milton, in short, has hardened the heart of the God that hardened Pharaoh's heart, and has narrowed his love and his power.

Some kind of internal blindness must have visited him if he did not perceive what must inevitably be the effect of all this on the sympathies and interest of the reader. And the irony of the thing is that his own sympathies were not proof against the trial that he had devised for them. He lavished all his power, all his skill, and, in spite of himself, the greater part of his sympathy, on the splendid figure of Satan. He avoids calling *Para-*

dise Lost " an heroic poem " ; when it was printed, in 1667, the title-page ran merely—*Paradise Lost, A Poem in Ten Books.* Had he inserted the word "heroic," the question as to who is the hero would have been broached at once. And to that question, if it be fairly faced, only one answer can be given,—the answer that has already been given by Dryden and Goethe, by Lord Chesterfield and Professor Masson. It was not for nothing that Milton stultified the professed moral of his poem, and emptied it of all spiritual content. He was not fully conscious, it seems, of what he was doing ; but he builded better than he knew. A profound poetic instinct taught him to preserve epic truth at all costs. And the epic value of *Paradise Lost* is centred in the character and achievements of Satan.

Satan unavoidably reminds us of Prometheus, and although there are essential differences, we are not made to feel them essential. His very situation as the fearless antagonist of Omnipotence makes him either a fool or a hero, and Milton is far indeed from permitting us to think him a fool. The nobility and greatness of his bearing are brought home to us in some half-dozen of the finest poetic passages in the world. The most stupendous of the poet's imaginative creations are made the foil for a greater than themselves. Was ever terror more magnificently embodied than in the phantom figure of Death ?—

> The other Shape—
> If shape it might be called that shape had none
> Distinguishable in member, joint, or limb ;
> Or substance might be called that shadow seemed,
> For each seemed either—black it stood as Night,
> Fierce as ten Furies, terrible as Hell,
> And shook a dreadful dart : what seemed his head
> The likeness of a kingly crown had on.
> Satan was now at hand, and from his seat
> The monster moving onward came as fast
> With horrid strides ; Hell trembled as he strode.

This is the passage that drew from Burke a rapture of praise. But as it stands in the poem its elevation is a scaffolding merely, whence we may view the greatness of Satan :—

> The undaunted Fiend what this might be admired—
> Admired, not feared (God and his Son except,
> Created thing naught valued he nor shunned).

The same magnificent effect of suggestion is wrought even more subtly in the scene where Satan approaches
> the throne
> Of *Chaos*, and his dark pavilion spread
> Wide on the wasteful Deep.

Courteously and fearlessly Satan addresses himself to the monarch of the nethermost abyss. His speech contains no threats ; he asks guidance in his quest ; and, with politic forethought, promises that that quest, if successful, shall restore an outlying lost province to Chaos. There is nothing

in his words to cause consternation ; but the King
is afraid :—

> Him thus the anarch old,
> With faltering speech and visage incomposed,
> Answered :—" I know thee, stranger, who thou art—
> That mighty leading Angel, who of late
> Made head against Heaven's King, though overthrown."

In the war on the plains of Heaven Satan ranges
up and down the fighting line, like Cromwell ;
he fortifies his comrades to endurance, and en-
courages them to attack. In Hell he stands like
a tower :—

> His form had yet not lost
> All her original brightness, nor appeared
> Less than Archangel ruined, and the excess
> Of glory obscured.

In his contests with Michael in Heaven and with
Gabriel on Earth he never falls below himself :—

> " If I must contend," said he,
> " Best with the best—the sender, not the sent ;
> Or all at once."

But his motive passions, it is objected, were
envy, ambition, and hate, and his end was a crime.
To which objection a modern poet has replied
that a crime will serve as a measure for the spirit.
Certainly to Satan there could never be imputed
the sin of " the unlit lamp and the ungirt loin."
And Milton has not left him devoid of the
gentlest passion, the passion of pity :—

> Cruel his eye, but cast
> Signs of remorse and passion, to behold
> The fellows of his crime, the followers rather
> (Far other once beheld in bliss), condemned
> For ever now to have their lot in pain—
> Millions of Spirits for his fault amerced
> Of Heaven, and from eternal splendours flung
> For his revolt—yet faithful how they stood,
> Their glory withered.

Thrice he attempts to address them, and thrice—

> in spite of scorn
> Tears, such as Angels weep, burst forth.

His followers are devotedly attached to him;
they admire him "that for the general safety he
despised his own"; and the only scene of rejoicing recorded in the annals of Hell, before the
Fall of Man, is at the dissolution of the Stygian
Council, when the devils come forth "rejoicing
in their matchless Chief."

As if of set purpose to raise Satan high above
the heads of the other Archangels, Milton devises
a pair of similar scenes, in Heaven and in Hell.
In the one Satan takes upon himself the unknown
dangers of the enterprise that has been approved
by the assembly. In the other, which occurs in
the very next book, the Heavenly Powers are
addressed from the Throne, and asked—

> "Which of ye will be mortal, to redeem
> Man's mortal crime, and just, the unjust to save?

Dwells in all Heaven charity so dear ? "
  He asked, but all the Heavenly Quire stood mute,
And silence was in Heaven : on Man's behalf
Patron or intercessor none appeared—
Much less that durst upon his own head draw
The deadly forfeiture, and ransom set.

No wonder that Landor — although in another place he declares that Adam is the hero of *Paradise Lost*, and that "there is neither truth nor wit" in giving that name to Satan—is nevertheless startled by this passage into the comment, "I know not what interest Milton could have had in making Satan so august a creature, and so ready to share the dangers and sorrows of the angels he had seduced. I know not, on the other hand, what could have urged him to make the better ones so dastardly that even at the voice of their Creator not one among them offered his service to rescue from eternal perdition the last and weakest of intellectual beings."

When Satan first comes in sight of Paradisal bliss and the new-created pair, here surely was a chance for attributing to him the foul passions of envy and hate unalloyed? On the contrary, he is struck with admiration for their grace and infused divinity. He could love and pity them—so he muses — though himself unpitied. He seeks alliance with them, and is prepared to give them a share in all he has—which, it must be allowed, is the spirit of true hospitality. He feels it beneath him to attack innocence and helplessness, but public reasons compel him to do what otherwise he would abhor :—

> So spake the Fiend, and with necessity,
> The tyrant's plea, excused his devilish deeds.

But no imputation is cast on the sincerity of the plea, and we are left to conceive of Satan as of a lover of beauty reluctantly compelled to shatter it in the pursuit of his high political aims. In the same way, when he finds Eve alone, on the morning of the temptation, he is disarmed by her beauty and innocence, and, for a spell, is struck " stupidly good." Truly, Adam might boast, with Gibbon, that he fell by a noble hand.

It is possible that by the time he had completed the Fourth Book, Milton became uneasy as to the effect he was producing. Up to that point magnanimity and courage had been almost the monopoly of Satan. He had been the Great Dissenter, the undaunted and considerate leader of an outcast minority. But now, in the description of the war in Heaven, there came a chance of doing something to right the balance. Milton makes the most of the episode of Abdiel, who has been led away with the rest of Satan's followers, upon false pretences, and who, when he discovers the true purpose of the expedition, makes a lonely stand for the right :—

> Among the faithless faithful only he ; . . .
> Nor number nor example with him wrought
> To swerve from truth, or change his constant mind,
> Though single.

And Abdiel, when he meets Satan again after the outbreak of the war, glories in his nonconformity, and hisses out defiance :—

> Thou seest
> All are not of thy train ; there be who faith
> Prefer, and piety to God, though then
> To thee not visible when I alone
> Seemed in thy world erroneous to dissent
> From all : my Sect thou seest ; now learn too late
> How few sometimes may know when thousands err.

In this way Milton attempted to allay his scruples, and to divide the honours of dissent. Later on, after the Fall, when Satan returns to Hell with tidings of his exploit, the change of all the devils to serpents, and of their applause to "a dismal universal hiss" was perhaps devised to cast a slur upon the success of his mission. Some critics have professed to discern a certain progressive degradation and shrinkage in Satan as the poem proceeds. But his original creation lived on in the imagination and memory of Milton, and was revived, with an added pathos, in *Paradise Regained*. The most moving of all Satan's speeches is perhaps the long pleading there made in answer to the challenge of Christ, and its tone of unutterable despair is deepened by the terrible severity of the speech made in answer.

The other leaders of the rebel troops take little part in the action outside the scene of the Infernal Council. In his memories of the Long Parliament Milton could easily find examples of the types he has embodied under the names of Belial, Mammon, Moloch, and Beelzebub. Nor has he forgotten the Westminster Assembly of divines. The precise employments of that historic body are described by him as the recreation of the lost spirits :—

> Others apart sat on a hill retired,
> In thoughts more elevate, and reasoned high
> Of Providence, Foreknowledge, Will, and Fate—
> Fixed fate, free will, foreknowledge absolute—
> And found no end, in wandering mazes lost.

It ill became Milton to cast contempt on these reasonings, seeing that a whole system of them was necessary for the argument of his poem. He is so little of a philosopher that he seems hardly to be conscious of the difficulties of his own theory. Both in *Paradise Lost* and in the *Treatise of Christian Doctrine* he enlarges with much dogmatism and some arrogance on the difference between foreknowledge and foreordination. He rejects predestination decisively, but he not only does not answer, he does not even so much as mention, the difficulty that arises in attempting to distinguish between what is foreordained by Omniscience and what is foreknown by Omnipotence. Pope compared some of the speeches delivered in Heaven to the arguments of a "School-divine." The comparison does injustice to the scholastic philosophers. There was never one of them who could have walked into a metaphysical bramble - bush with the blind recklessness that Milton displays.

It is time to return to Eden and its inhabitants. They have little to do but " to lop and prune and prop and bind," to adore their Maker, and to avoid the prohibited tree. It would perhaps have been impossible for a poet with more dramatic genius than Milton to make these favourites of Heaven interesting in their happy state, while yet the key that was to admit them to our world of adventure and experience, of suffering and achievement, hung untouched on a tree. And Adam, from the wealth of his inexperience, is lavishly sententious ; when anything is to do, even if it is only to go to sleep, he does it in a high style, and makes a speech. Milton plainly saw the danger of arousing a sense of incongruity and ludicrous disproportion from the contest between these harmless tame creatures and the great forces of Satan's empire. So he makes man strong in innocence, and, unlike the fallen angels, exempt from all physical pain or wound. He even goes so far as to make Satan afraid of Adam, of his heroic build and intellectual power. This last, it might be said, is a fear not explained by anything that we are privileged to hear from the lips of Adam himself; but perhaps, in the case of our great ancestor, we shall do well to remember Hamlet's advice to the players, "Follow that lord, and look you mock him not."

There remains a more important person—Eve. And with Eve, since the beginning of Milton criticism, there enter all those questions concerning the comparative worthiness and the relative authority of husband and wife which critics of Milton so often and so gladly step aside to discuss. Every one knows the line :—

> He for God only, she for God in him.

Almost every one knows the lines :—

> Nothing lovelier can be found
> In woman than to study household good,
> And good works in her husband to promote.

Milton certainly shared the views of Knox concerning the "Monstrous Regiment of Women." It is unnecessary to meet him on his own ground, or to attempt a theory that shall explain or control Eve, Cleopatra, Joan of Arc, Catherine of the Medici, Mary Powell, and others of their sex. Such theories prove only that man is a generalising and rationalising animal. The poet brought his fate on himself, for since Eve was the mother of mankind, he thought fit to make her the embodiment of a doctrine. But he also (a thing of far deeper interest) coloured his account by the introduction of personal memories and feelings. Of Eve, at least, he never writes indifferently. When he came to write *Samson Agonistes*, the intensity of his feelings concerning Dalila caused him to deviate from the best Greek tradition and to assign inappropriate matter to the Chorus. And even in his matter-of-fact *History of Britain*, the name of Boadicea awakens him to a fit of indignation with the Britons who upheld her rule. There is full scope in *Paradise Lost* for similar expressions of indignation. Adam, after the Fall, speaks of his wife as

> Not to be trusted—longing to be seen,
> Though by the Devil himself.

In the Eleventh Book the daughters of men are described as bred only

> to sing, to dance,
> To dress, and troll the tongue, and roll the eye.

But Milton, it is sometimes forgotten, was also the author of that beautiful eulogy of Eve in the Eighth Book :—

> When I approach
> Her loveliness, so absolute she seems
> And in herself complete, so well to know

Her own, that what she wills to do or say
Seems wisest, virtuousest, discreetest, best.
All higher Knowledge in her presence falls
Degraded ; Wisdom in discourse with her
Loses, discountenanced, and like Folly shows ;
Authority and Reason on her wait,
As one intended first, not after made
Occasionally ; and, to consummate all,
Greatness of mind and nobleness their seat
Build in her loveliest, and create an awe
About her, as a guard angelic placed.

It is an exact parallel to Florizel's praise of
Perdita in *The Winter's Tale* :—

When you speak, sweet,
I'd have you do it ever : when you sing,
I'd have you buy and sell so, so give alms,
Pray so ; and, for the ordering your affairs,
To sing them too ; when you do dance, I wish you
A wave o' the sea, that you might ever do
Nothing but that ; move still, still so,
And own no other function : each your doing,
So singular in each particular,
Crowns what you are doing in the present deed,
That all your acts are queens.

But Florizel addresses his praise to the lady herself ;
while Adam, who had never been young, confides
it in private to Raphael, after dinner, and studies
a more instructive and authoritative strain in his
conversations with Eve. And now comes a point
worthy of remark. The Angel, to whom, it
cannot be doubted, Milton committed the exposi-

tion of his own views, after hearing this confession, frowns, and administers a tart reproof. He describes Eve, somewhat grudgingly, as "an outside—fair, no doubt," and peremptorily teaches Adam the duties of self-appreciation and self-assertion :—

> Oft-times nothing profits more
> Than self-esteem, grounded on just and right
> Well managed. Of that skill the more thou know'st,
> The more she will acknowledge thee her head,
> And to realities yield all her shows.

And in the sequel, Adam bitterly laments that he had failed to profit by this advice. He might have been comforted by the wisdom of Chaucer's Franklin :—

> When maistrie cometh, the god of love anon
> Beteth his wynges and, farewel, he is gon !

The explanation of all this is clear to see. Milton was not, as he has sometimes been described, a callous and morose Puritan. He was extraordinarily susceptible to the attractions of feminine beauty and grace. Adam's confession is his own. But the ideal of character that he had put before himself caused him passionately to resent this susceptibility. It was the joint in his harness, the main breach in his Stoicism, the great anomaly in a life regulated as for his Task-master. He felt that beauty was a power not himself, un-balancing and disturbing the rational self-centred poise of his soul. There have been poets whose service of Venus Verticordia was whole-hearted. But to Milton the power of Beauty was a magnetism to be distrusted for its very strength. He felt something of what he makes Satan express, that there is terror in love and beauty "not approached by stronger hate." The Chorus in *Samson Agonistes* makes a similar observation :—

> Yet beauty, though injurious, hath strange power
> After offence returning, to regain
> Love once possessed.

To escape from the dominion of the tyrant is the duty of a wise man. When Raphael remarked that "Love . . . hath his seat in Reason, and is judicious," he committed himself to a statement which a longer experience of the world would have enabled him to correct. But Milton wished it true ; and perhaps even lured himself into a belief of its truth. At any rate, when Satan, in *Paradise Regained*, expounds his opinion on the matter, it is found, for once, to be in substantial agreement with Raphael's :—

> Beauty stands
> In the admiration only of weak minds
> Led captive ; cease to admire, and all her plumes
> Fall flat, and shrink into a trivial toy,
> At every sudden slighting quite abashed.

It is a great loss to literature that Mrs.

Millamant, the delightful heroine of Congreve's comedy, was no reader of Milton. Her favourite author was Suckling :—

> I prithee spare me, gentle boy,
> Press me no more for that slight toy,
> That foolish trifle of a heart.

If she had a copy of the *Paradise Regained*, doubtless it stood in some conspicuous place, and was never opened,—like Mrs. Wishfort's " books over the chimney—Quarles and Prynne, and ' The Short View of the Stage,' with Bunyan's works, to entertain you." But all unawares she has answered the contention of Satan :—" O the vanity of these men !—Fainall, d'ye hear him ? If they did not commend us, we were not handsome ! Now you must know that they could not commend one, if one was not handsome. Beauty the lover's gift !— Lord, what is a lover, that it can give ? . . . One no more owes one's beauty to a lover than one's wit to an echo."

Like most men of an impressionable temperament and a strong will, Milton was not sympathetic, nor curious to place himself where he might see the world from a point of view other than his own. Besieged by their sensations and impressions, concerned above all things with maintaining their opinions and enforcing their beliefs on others, such men find enough to do within the citadel of their own personality. To judge from some passages of his works, one half of the human race was to Milton an illusion to which the other half was subject. One who is in love with his own ideas cannot but be disappointed alike with existing institutions and with the tissue of surprises that is a person. Milton's disappointment, which had inspired the early Divorce pamphlets, finds renewed expression in Adam's prophecy of unhappy marriages — a notable parallel to the similar prophecy in *Venus and Adonis*—

> For either
> He never shall find out fit mate, but such
> As some misfortune brings him, or mistake ;
> Or whom he wishes most shall seldom gain,
> Through her perverseness, but shall see her gained
> By a far worse ; or, if she love, withheld
> By parents ; or his happiest choice too late
> Shall meet, already linked and wedlock-bound
> To a fell adversary, his hate or shame.

But, with all this, of our two grand parents Eve is the better drawn and the more human. Milton did not intend that it should be so, but he could not help it. One consequence of the doctrine—

> He for God only, she for God in him—

is that Adam's single impulse of unselfishness, whereby he elects to share the offence and punishment of Eve, is a vice in him, a " bad compliance." Self-abnegation, the duty of Eve, is hardly within the right of Adam; and Dr. Johnson expressed a half-truth in violently paradoxical terms when he said that Milton " thought woman made only for obedience and man only for rebellion." It would be truer, and weaker, to say that Milton thought woman made for the exercise of private, and man for the exercise of public, virtues. Hence in their mutual relations Eve carries off all the honours, for her duty towards Adam coincides with her inclination, while in his case the two are at variance. There is no speech of Adam's to be matched with the pleading intensity of Eve's appeal, beginning—"Forsake me not thus, Adam!"—and to her Milton commits the last and best speech spoken in Paradise:—

> But now lead on ;
> In me is no delay ; with thee to go
> Is to stay here ; without thee here to stay
> Is to go hence unwilling ; thou to me
> Art all things under Heaven, all places thou,
> Who for my wilful crime art banished hence.

She is generous and loving ; her only reproach addressed to Adam is that he acceded to her request, and permitted her, on that fateful morning, to do her gardening alone, among the roses and myrtles. She is a fair companion picture to set over against Dalila, and is utterly incapable of Dalila's hypocrisy in justifying private treachery by reasons of public

policy. There is even a certain dramatic development in her character ; after she has eaten of the
fruit, audacity and deceit appear in her reflections ;
she meditates withholding from Adam the advan-
tages of the tree, in order that she may become—

> More equal, and perhaps—
> A thing not undesirable—sometimes
> Superior.

It is easy to understand how tired Eve might well
become (even before the fallacious fruit was tasted)
of Adam's carefully maintained superiority. On
thinking, however, of the judgment that she may
have to suffer, and of her own death, she resolves
to draw him in, her motive being not fear, but a
sudden movement of jealousy at the thought of—

> Adam wedded to another Eve.

This is as near an approach to drama in the handling of a human situation as is to be found in all
Paradise Lost.

But enough of this vein of criticism, which is
justified only by the pleasure of detecting Milton
too imperfectly concealed behind his handiwork.
To treat the scenes he portrays as if analysis of
character were his aim, and truth of psychology
his touchstone, is to do a wrong to the artist. He
is an epic, not a dramatic, poet ; to find him at his
best we must look at those passages of unsurpassed
magnificence wherein he describes some noble or

striking attitude, some strong or majestic action,
in its outward physical aspect.

In this, the loftiest part of his task, his other
defects, as if by some hidden law of compensation,
are splendidly redeemed.   While he deals with
abstract thought or moral truth his handling is
tight, pedantic, and disagreeably hard.   But when
he comes to describe his epic personages and his
embodied visions, all is power, and vagueness, and
grandeur..   His imagination, escaped from the
narrow prison of his thought, rises like a vapour,
and, taking shape before his eyes, proclaims itself
his master.

No other poet has known so well how to portray,
in a few strokes, effects of multitude and vastness.
Now it is the sacred congregation in Heaven :—

> About him all the Sanctities of Heaven
> Stood thick as stars, and from his sight received
> Beatitude past utterance.

Now the warrior host of Hell :—

> He spake ; and, to confirm his words, outflew
> Millions of flaming swords, drawn from the thighs
> Of mighty Cherubim ; the sudden blaze
> Far round illumined Hell.

In these, as in other like scenes, he preserves epic
unity by throwing the whole into the distance.
So after the approach of the Messiah to battle,
" the poet," says Coleridge, " by one touch from

himself—'far off their coming shone!'—makes the whole one image." He describes at a greater range of vision than any other poet : the frame-work of his single scenes is often not less than a third of universal space. When he has added figure to figure in the endeavour to picture the multitudinous disarray of the fallen Angels on the lake, one line suffices to reduce the whole spectacle to its due dimensions beneath that cavernous tent of darkness :—

> He called so loud that all the hollow deep
> Of Hell resounded.

The same effect of number and vastness, diminished and unified by the same reference to a larger setting, wherein all is seen at a glance, may be noted in the description of the raising of Satan's standard in Hell :—

> The imperial ensign, which, full high advanced,
> Shone like a meteor streaming to the wind,
> With gems and golden lustre rich emblazed,
> Seraphic arms and trophies ; all the while
> Sonorous metal blowing martial sounds :
> At which the universal host up-sent
> A shout that tore Hell's concave, and beyond
> Frighted the reign of Chaos and old Night.
> All in a moment through the gloom were seen
> Ten thousand banners rise into the air,
> With orient colours waving : with them rose
> A forest huge of spears ; and thronging helms
> Appeared, and serried shields in thick array
> Of depth immeasureable.

Sometimes a line or two gives him scope enough for the rendering of one of these epic scenes, immense and vivid. The ruin and prostration of the rebels is made visible in two lines :—

> Cherub and Seraph rolling in the flood
> With scattered arms and ensigns.

And the picture of the East rises at a touch :—

> Dusk faces with white silken turbants wreathed.

In the drawing of single attitudes Milton studies the same large decorum and majesty. He is never tempted into detail in the describing of gesture or action ; never loses the whole in the part. The bulk of *Paradise Lost* was written between the sixth and the thirteenth years of his blindness. Since the veil had fallen he had lived with the luminous shapes that he could picture against the dark. The human face had lost, in his recollection of it, something of its minuter delineation, but nothing of its radiance. On the other hand, the human figure, in its most significant gestures and larger movements, haunted his visions. His description of the appearance of the wife whom he had never seen is an early model of many of his later drawings. She comes to his bedside and leans over him, stretching forth her arms :

> Her face was veiled ; yet to my fancied sight
> Love, sweetness, goodness, in her person shined
> So clear as in no face with more delight.

Adam and Eve, as they are first seen in Paradise, have the same shining quality, the same vagueness of beauty expressing itself in purely emotional terms. Satan standing on the top of Mount Niphates, looking down on Eden spread out at his feet, and then with fierce gesticulation addressing himself to the sun at the zenith, is one of the dim solitary figures that dwell in the mind's eye. No less impressive and no less indefinite are those two monumental descriptions of the rebel leader ; the first, of his going forth to war in Heaven :—

> High in the midst, exalted as a God,
> The Apostate in his sun-bright chariot sat,
> Idol of majesty divine, enclosed
> With flaming Cherubim and golden shields.

and the other, of his encounter with Gabriel :—

> Satan, alarmed,
> Collecting all his might, dilated stood,
> Like Teneriff or Atlas, unremoved :
> His stature reached the sky, and on his crest
> Sat Horror plumed ; nor wanted in his grasp
> What seemed both spear and shield.

In these, and in a hundred other notable passages, the images are as simple and broad as the emotional effects that they produce,—the sun, flame, gold, a mountain, the sky.

Some of the scenes and situations delineated by Milton are of a gentler and more elusive virtue than these terrors and sublimities. His descriptions of morning and evening are always charged with emotion—the quiet coming-on of night in Eden ; or the break of day in the wilderness of the Temptation, with a sense of joy and relief " after a night of storm so ruinous." His feeling for the imaginative effects of architecture in a landscape is extraordinarily subtle. One, at least, of these effects is hardly to be experienced among the hedgerows and farmsteads and placid rambling towns of England. Travellers in Italy, or in the East, are better able to understand the transfiguration of a landscape by the distant view of a small compact array of walls and towers perched on a vantage-ground among the hills of the horizon. The lawlessness of Nature, the homelessness of the surface of the earth, and the fears that haunt uninhabited places, are all accentuated by the distrust that frowns from the battlements of such a stronghold of militant civility. For this reason, perhaps, the architectural features in certain pictures and drawings have an indescribable power of suggestion. The city, self-contained and fortified, overlooking a wide expanse of country, stands for safety and society ; the little group of figures, parleying at the gate, or moving down into the plain, awakens in the mind a sense of far-off things,—the moving accidents of the great outer world, and the dangers and chances of the unknown. Bunyan, whose

imagination was nourished on the Eastern scenery and sentiment of the Bible, shows himself powerfully affected by situations of this kind, as where, in the beginning of the *Pilgrim's Progress*, he describes the man with his face from his own home, running from the City of Destruction, and the group of his kindred calling after him to return :—
" but the man put his fingers in his ears, and ran on crying, Life, Life, Eternal Life : so he looked not behind him, but fled towards the middle of the plain."

Such another figure is Milton's Abdiel, who escaped from the rebel citadel—

> And with retorted scorn his back he turned
> On those proud towers, to swift destruction doomed.

The perils of his flight are vaguely indicated by a few admirable touches in the opening of the next Book :—

All night the dreadless Angel, unpursued,
Through Heaven's wide champaign held his way, till Morn
Waked by the circling Hours, with rosy hand
Unbarred the gates of Light.

A more signal instance of the same poetic effect is to be found in the wonderful close of *Paradise Lost*, where Adam and Eve are led down from the garden by the archangel Michael, and are left standing in the vast plain below :—

They, looking back, all the eastern side beheld
Of Paradise, so late their happy seat,
Waved over by that flaming brand ; the gate
With dreadful faces thronged and fiery arms.
Some natural tears they dropped, but wiped them soon ;
The world was all before them, where to choose
Their place of rest, and Providence their guide.
They, hand in hand, with wandering steps and slow,
Through Eden took their solitary way.

Criticism might exhaust itself in the effort to do justice to the beauty of this close. Of Adam and Eve it may be truly said that none of all their doings in the garden became them like the leaving of it. Yet Addison and Bentley, the ornaments of a polite and learned age, are at one in their depreciation of the last two lines. Addison, after a formal apology for "the smallest Alteration in this divine Work," boldly recommends amputation ; while Bentley, with the caution of a more experienced surgeon, offers to crutch the lines on certain wooden contrivances of his own. The three epithets, "wandering," "slow," and "solitary," are all censured by him. Our first parents, he remarks, were guided by Providence, and therefore needed not to wander ; they were reassured by Michael's predictions, and so might well display an engaging briskness ; while as for "their solitary way," they were no more solitary than in Paradise, "there being no Body besides Them Two, both here and there."

He therefore suggests a distich more agreeable to the general scheme :—

> Then hand in hand with social steps their way
> Through Eden took, with Heav'nly Comfort cheer'd.

It is impossible to answer such criticism; the organs of human speech are too frail. Let Bentley be left to contemplate with delight the hideous gash that his chopper has inflicted on the Miltonic rhythm of the last line. If Addison, for his part, had been less concerned with the opinions of M. Bossu, and the enumeration of the books of the *Æneid*, he might have found leisure to notice that the two later poems, *Paradise Regained* and *Samson Agonistes*, are each brought to a close which exactly resembles the close of *Paradise Lost*. After the splendours in the last book of *Paradise Regained*—the fall of Satan, "smitten with amazement," from the pinnacle of the Temple, the elaborate classical comparisons of Antaeus and the Sphinx, and the triumphal chorus of Angels who bear the Son of God aloft with anthems of victory—the poem ends with the same exquisite lull :—

> He, unobserved,
> Home to his mother's house private returned.

And *Samson Agonistes* brings as glorious a triumph to no less peaceful a close :—

> And calm of mind, all passion spent.

The dying fall is the same in all three, and is the form of ending preferred by the musical and poetic genius of Milton.

Passages of a crowded and ostentatious magnificence are more frequent in *Paradise Lost* than in either of the two later poems. In *Paradise Regained* and *Samson Agonistes* the enhanced severity of a style which rejects almost all ornament was due in part, no doubt, to a gradual change in Milton's temper and attitude. It is not so much that his power of imagination waned, as that his interest veered, turning more to thought and reflection, less to action and picture. In these two poems, at the last, he celebrated that

> better fortitude
> Of patience and heroic martyrdom

which he had professed to sing in *Paradise Lost*. We are told by his nephew that he " could not bear with patience any such thing related to him " as that *Paradise Regained* was inferior to *Paradise Lost*. He was right ; its merits and beauties are of a different and more sombre kind, yet of a kind perhaps further out of the reach of any other poet than even the constellated glories of *Paradise Lost* itself. It should be remembered that *Paradise Lost*, although it was written by Milton between the fiftieth and the fifty-seventh years of his age, was conceived by him, in its main outlines,

not later than his thirty - fourth year. Two of
the passages noticed above, where Satan addresses
himself to the Sun and where the Angel leads
Adam and Eve out of Paradise, embody situations
which had appealed to his younger imagination.
Some of the very words of Satan's address were
written, we learn from Phillips, about 1642. And
the expulsion of Adam and Eve seems to contain
a reminiscence of the time when Milton was considering the history of Lot as a possible subject for
an epic. The lines—

> In either hand the hastening Angel caught
> Our lingering parents—

were perhaps suggested by the Scripture narrative
—"And while he lingered, the men laid hold
upon his hand, and upon the hand of his wife,
. . . and they brought him forth, and set him
without the city" (Genesis xix. 16).

The gravity and density of the style of
Paradise Lost would have been beyond the power
of youth, even of the youth of Milton ; but the
action of the poem, with all its vividness and
vigour, could perhaps hardly have been first conceived in mature age. The composition was long
deferred, so that in the decade which witnessed the
production of all three great poems we see a
strangely rapid development, or change rather, of
manner. In *Paradise Lost* Milton at last delivered

himself of the work that had been brooding over him "with mighty wings outspread" during all the years of his manhood. But his imagination could not easily emancipate itself from that over-mastering presence ; and when he took up with a fresh task he gladly chose a theme closely related to the theme of *Paradise Lost*, and an opportunity of re-introducing some of the ancient figures. A kind-hearted, simple-minded, pig-headed young Quaker, called Thomas Ellwood, takes to himself credit for having suggested a sequel to the story of the Fall. "Thou hast said much here," he re-marked to Milton, "of *Paradise Lost;* but what hast thou to say of *Paradise Found?*" The words, as it seemed to Ellwood, sank deep, and did their work. "He made me no answer, but sate some time in a muse, then brake off that dis-course and fell upon another subject." Perhaps while he sat in a muse Milton was attempting to sound, with the plummet of conjecture, the abyss of human folly, "dark, wasteful, wild." So early as in the fourth line of *Paradise Lost*, and already very fully in the Third Book, he had treated of *Paradise Found* as an integral part of his subject. The episode of the Eleventh and Twelfth Books was wholly concerned with it. It seems not unlikely, however, that he caught at the suggestion as an excuse for a new and independent work. One of the commonest kinds of critical stupidity is the kind that discovers something "unfinished" in a great work of art, and suggests desirable trimmings and additions. Milton knew that *Paradise Lost* was finished, in every sense. But room had not been found in it for all that now held the chief place in his matured thought. When he chose the theme of his great work, the actual temptation of man probably bulked much larger in his design than it does in the completed poem. His epic creatures, from being the machinery of the poem, usurped a share of the control. With all Milton's care and skill, there is very little interest in the actual plucking of the apple ; Eve was too simple a pleader to make much of the case for the defence. Yet human life presented itself to Milton chiefly under the guise of a series of temptations. The title of one of Andrew Marvell's pieces might well be used to describe the whole canon of his poetry, from *L'Allegro* to *Samson Agonistes*—all are parts of *A Dialogue between the Resolved Soul and Created Pleasure*. To his youthful fancy Mirth and Melancholy present themselves in the likeness of rival goddesses, claiming allegiance, and offering gifts. The story of Samson is a story of temptation, yielded to through weakness, punished by ignominy, and, in the end, magnificently expiated. In *Comus* is shown how the temptations of created pleasure may be resisted by the chastity of the "resolved soul." In *Paradise Lost*, however, the resolved soul had somehow, failing Man, found for itself a congenial habitation in the Devil. The high and pure philosophy of the Lady and her brothers has no counterpart in the later and greater poem. Milton, therefore, willingly seized on the suggestion made by Ellwood; and in *Paradise Regained* exhibited at length, with every variety of form and argument, the spectacle of—

> one man's firm obedience fully tried
> Through all temptation, and the Tempter foiled
> In all his wiles, defeated and repulsed.

The subject of *Comus* is repeated; but in place of the dazzling allurement of the senses which is the temptation of the earlier poem, there is the temptation of the will, the appeal made in vain by Satan to those more strenuous and maturer passions of pride, ambition, love of wealth, and love of power. Instead of the innocent and instinctive purity of the Lady, which unmasks the fallacies of Comus, there is heard in *Paradise Regained* the voice of a high Stoical philosophy, strong in self-sufficiency, rich in illustrations drawn from the experience of the ages, and attributed, by this singular poet, to the Christ.

If his only purpose had been to make a worthy epical counterpart to *Paradise Lost*, those critics are doubtless right who think his chosen subject not altogether adequate to the occasion. The Fall of Man is best matched by the Redemption of Man—a subject which Milton, whether he knew it or not, was particularly ill-qualified to treat. It is sketched, hastily and prosaically, in the Twelfth Book of *Paradise Lost*; but there is no escaping from the conclusion that the central mystery of the Christian religion occupied very little space in Milton's scheme of religion and thought. Had he chosen this subject, the account given, in the apocryphal Gospel of Nicodemus, of the Descent into Hell might have furnished him with rich material for one part of his theme. The conquest of the upper world by Satan, narrated in *Paradise Lost*, might have had for natural sequel the triumphant descent into Hell of the King of Glory, and the liberation of the captives. For Milton's grandiose epical vein the theme has great opportunities, as a brief summary of the Gospel of Nicodemus will show :—

Karinus and Leucius, sons of Simeon, being raised from the dead, write what occurred during their sojourn in the realm of Hades : " While we were lying, along with our fathers, in the depth of the pit and in the uttermost darkness, suddenly there appeared the golden hue of the sun, and a purple royal light shining in upon us. Then the father of all mankind and all the patriarchs and prophets rejoiced, saying : ' That light is the author of everlasting light, who hath promised to translate us to everlasting light.' And Isaiah cried out, and said : ' This is the Light of the Father, the Son of God, according to my prophecy that I prophesied when I was alive upon the earth, " The land of Zabulon, and the land of Nephthalim, beyond Jordan ; the people which sat in darkness saw a great light, and to them which sat in the region and shadow of death light is sprung up." And now he has come, and has shone upon us who are sitting in death.'

Then Simeon spoke in a like strain of exultation. John the Baptist arrived, a herald of the King of Glory ; and Seth, at the bidding of Adam, told how Michael the Archangel had refused him oil from the tree of mercy for the anointing of the body of Adam when he was sick, and had comforted him with the assurance that when the years should be fulfilled Adam would be raised up again, and led into Paradise.

And even while the saints were rejoicing there broke out dissension among the lords of Hell. Satan, boasting of his latest exploit, told Hades, the prince of Hell, how he had led Jesus of Nazareth captive to death. But Hades was ill satisfied and asked, ' Perchance this is the same Jesus who by the word of his command took away Lazarus after he had been four days in corruption, whom I kept as dead ? ' And Satan answered and

said, 'It is the same.' And when Hades heard
this he said to him, 'I adjure thee by thy powers
and mine, bring him not to me. For when I
heard the power of his word I trembled for fear,
and all my officers were struck with amazement.'
And while they were thus disputing, suddenly
there was a voice as of thunder, and a shouting as
of a multitude of spirits, saying, 'Lift up your
gates, O ye princes, and be ye lifted up, ye everlasting gates, and the King of Glory shall come in.'
Then Hades, hearing this, said to Satan, 'Depart
from me, and get thee out of my realm ; if thou
art a powerful warrior, fight against the King of
Glory.' And he cast him forth from his habitations.

And while David and Isaiah were speaking,
recalling the words of their prophecy, there came
to Hell, in the form of a man, the Lord of
Majesty, and lighted up the eternal darkness, and
burst asunder the indissoluble chains, and seizing
Satan delivered him over to the power of Hades,
but Adam he drew with him to his brightness.

Then Hades receiving Satan reviled him
vehemently and said, 'O Prince of perdition, and
author of extermination, derision of angels and
scorn of the just, why didst thou do this thing?
All thy riches which thou hast acquired by the
tree of transgression and the loss of Paradise, thou
hast now lost by the tree of the cross, and all thy
joy has perished.'

But the Lord, holding Adam by the hand, delivered him to Michael the Archangel, and all the saints followed Michael the Archangel, and he led them into Paradise, filled with mercy and glory."

Milton would hardly have entertained for a moment the idea of a subject taken from one of the apocryphal gospels. And even if he had felt no scruples on this point, the theme of the Harrying of Hell would hardly have commended itself to him in his later years, least of all its triumphant close. His interest was now centred rather in the sayings of the wise than in the deeds of the mighty. The " crude apple that diverted Eve " was indeed a simple theme compared with the profound topics that are treated in *Samson Agonistes*. The dark tangle of human life ; the inscrutable course of Divine providence ; the punishment so unwittingly and lightly incurred, yet lying on a whole nation " heavy as frost, and deep almost as life " ; the temptation presenting itself in the guise neither of pleasure, nor of ambition, but of despair ; and, through all, the recurring assertion of unyielding trust and un- flinching acquiescence in the will of God ; the song of the Chorus—

> Just are the ways of God
> And justifiable to men—

finding an echo in Samson's declaration—

> Nothing of all these evils hath befallen me
> But justly ; I myself have brought them on ;
> Sole author I, sole cause ;

—these together make up a theme where there is no possible place for the gay theology of *Paradise Lost.* The academic proof of God's justice, contained in the earlier poem, if it were introduced into *Samson Agonistes* could be met only with the irony of Job : " Am I a sea, or a sea-monster, that thou settest a watch over me ? . . . What is man, that thou shouldest magnify him, and that thou shouldest set thine heart upon him, and that thou shouldest visit him every morning, and try him every moment? " The question has become a real one ; not to be answered now by the dogmatism and dialectic of a system. Milton's bewilderment and distress of mind are voiced in the cry of the Chorus :—

> Yet toward these thus dignified thou oft
> Amidst their height of noon
> Changest thy countenance, and thy hand with no regard
> Of highest favours past
> From thee or them, or them to thee of service.

And there follows their humble prayer, heard and answered with Divine irony on the very day of their asking :—

> So deal not with this once thy glorious champion,
> The image of thy strength and mighty minister.
> What do I beg ? How hast thou dealt already ?

Behold him in this state calamitous, and turn
His labours, for thou canst, to peaceful end.

In the days that now, as he looked back on his
youth and manhood, must have seemed to him both
distant and barren, Milton had sought for triumph,
in action and in argument. His seeking was
denied him ; but he found peace, and the grace to
accept it.

CHAPTER V

To approach the question of Milton's poetic style thus late in the course of this treatise is to fall into the absurdity of the famous art-critic, who, lecturing on the Venus of Milo, devoted the last and briefest of his lectures to the shape of that noble work of art. In truth, since Milton died, his name is become the mark, not of a biography nor of a theme, but of a style—the most distinguished in our poetry. But the task of literary criticism is, at the best, a task of such disheartening difficulty, that those who attempt it should be humoured if they play long with the fringes of the subject, and wait for courageous moments to attack essentials.

In one sense, of course, and that not the least important, the great works of Milton were the product of the history and literatures of the world. Cycles ferried his cradle. Generations guided him. All forces were steadily employed to complete him.

But when we attempt to separate the single strands of his complex genealogy, to identify and arrange the influences that made him, the essential somehow escapes us. The genealogical method in literary history is both interesting and valuable, but we are too apt, in our admiration for its lucid procedure, to forget that there is one thing which it will never explain, and that thing is poetry. Books beget books ; but the mystery of conception still evades us. We display, as if in a museum, all the bits of thought and fragments of expression that Milton may have borrowed from Homer and Virgil, from Ariosto and Shakespeare. Here is a far-fetched conceit, and there is an elaborately jointed comparison. But these choice fragments and samples were to be had by any one for the taking ; what it baffles us to explain is how they came to be of so much more use to Milton than ever they were to us. In any dictionary of quotations you may find great thoughts and happy expressions as plentiful and as cheap as sand, and, for the most part, quite as useless. These are dead thoughts : to catalogue, compare, and arrange them is within the power of any competent literary workman ; but to raise them to blood-heat again, to breathe upon them and vitalise them is the sign that proclaims a poet. The ledger school of criticism, which deals only with borrowings and lendings, ingeniously traced and accurately recorded, looks foolish enough in the presence of this miracle. There is a sort of critics who, in effect, decry poetry, by fixing their attention solely on the possessions that poetry inherits. They are like Mammon—

> the least erected Spirit that fell
> From Heaven ; for even in Heaven his looks and thoughts
> Were always downward bent, admiring more
> The riches of Heaven's pavement, trodden gold,
> Than aught divine or holy else enjoyed
> In vision beatific.

With curious finger and thumb they pick holes in the mosaic ; and wherever there is wealth they are always ready to cry " Thief ! "

There is real interest in the enumeration of Milton's borrowings, and in the citation of parallel passages from the ancients to illustrate his work. But since style is the expression of a living organism, not a problem of cunning tesselation, it is permissible, in this place, to pass over what he borrowed from the ancients, in order to deal with a more intimate matter, and to attempt a valuation of which he borrowed from no one, either ancient or modern.

His indomitable personality and irrepressible originality have left their stamp on all his work, and have moulded his treatment, his handling, his diction, his style. We, who have been inured for centuries to Miltonic mouthings and manner-

isms, are too likely to underestimate the degree
of his originality. Coleridge was probably wrong
when he said that "Shakespeare's poetry is
characterless ; that is, it does not reflect the
individual Shakespeare." But he was unquestion-
ably right when he added that "John Milton
himself is in every line of *Paradise Lost.*" The
more they are studied, the more do Milton's life
and his art seem to cohere, and to express the
pride and the power of his character.

Consider first his choice of subject. Ever since
the Renaissance had swept modern poetry back to
the pagan world, some voices of protest had been
raised, some swimmers, rather bold than strong, had
attempted to stem the tide. Among the earliest
of these was Thomas Sternhold, Groom of the
Chamber to King Henry the Eighth. Inspired perhaps by the example of a better poet, Clement Marot,
Sternhold thrust some of the Psalms of David into
a carterly metre, "thinking thereby," says Anthony
a Wood, in his delightfully colloquial fashion,
"that the courtiers would sing them instead of
their sonnets, but did not, only some few excepted."
In the reign of Elizabeth, when the classical
mythology reigned and revelled in pageant and
masque, in court and town, one Thomas Brice, a
painful preacher, cried out against the pagan
fancies that had caught the English imagination
captive :—

We are not Ethnickes, we forsoth at least professe not so ;
Why range we then to Ethnickes' trade ?   Come back, where
    will ye go ?
Tel me, is Christe or Cupide lord ?   Doth God or Venus
    reign ?

But he cried to deaf ears, and the Elizabethan age
produced no body of sacred poetry worth a record.
The beautiful metrical version of the Psalms,
made by Sir Philip Sidney and his sister, remained
in manuscript for centuries.   Drayton's *Harmonie
of the Church* was suppressed.   Robert Southwell,
whose lyrics on sacred subjects give him a unique
place among the poets of his age, joins in the oft-
repeated complaint :—

> Stil finest wits are 'stilling Venus' rose,
> In Paynim toyes the sweetest vaines are spent ;
> To Christian workes few have their talents lent.

It was left for George Herbert and his contemporaries to take up the attempt once more—
this time with better success—"to reprove the
vanity of those many love poems that are daily
writ and consecrated to Venus, and to bewail that
so few are writ that look towards God and
heaven."

> Cannot thy dove
> Outstrip their Cupid easily in flight ?
> Or, since thy ways are deep, and still the same,
> Will not a verse run smooth that bears thy name ?

But although Herbert and his successors, in their

devotional lyrics, gave a whole new province to English poetry, they left the idolatrous government of the older provinces undisturbed. Dramatic and narrative poetry went on in the old way, and drew their inspiration from the old founts. Year by year, as our native poetic wealth increased, it became more and more difficult to break with the past, and to lead poetry back to Zion. Nature and precedent seemed allied against the innovation. The worst of religious poetry, as Johnson more than once pointed out, is its poverty of subject, and its enforced chastity of treatment. You cannot make a picture out of light alone ; there must be something to break it on. Then, too, there was Shakespeare to be reckoned with : he had written no hymns nor spiritual songs ; among the works of God, he had found man to be deserving of his unremitting attention ; yet, while a certain monotony of manner afflicted the singers of good and godly ballads, he had seemed never at a loss for a subject, never at the end of the copious inspiration that he drew from his unsanctified themes.

Nevertheless, the seventeenth century, which stirred so many questions in politics and criticism, stirred this also ; the fitness of sacred subjects for heroic poetry was debated long and ardently both in France and England, and many experiments were made. These experiments belong, as might be expected, mainly to the time of the civil troubles. It was then that the versifying of the Psalms became a desolating industry ; and Mr. Zachary Boyd, an ornament of the University of Glasgow, having worked his will on King David, made bold rhyming raids on passages of the Bible that are usually allowed to rest in prose. The high places of scholarship felt the new infection. Early in 1648, Joseph Beaumont, afterwards Master of Peterhouse, and Regius Professor of Divinity at Cambridge, published his poem called *Psyche, or Love's Mystery*, in twenty cantos. "My desire is," he says in the preface, "that this book may prompt better wits to believe that a divine theam is as capable and happy a subject of poetical ornament, as any pagan or humane device whatsoever." The poem is about four times as long as *Paradise Lost*, and was written in eleven months, which circumstance, his admiring biographer allows, "may create some surprise in a reader unacquainted with the vigorous imagination, and fertile flow of fancy, which so remarkably distinguished our author from the common class of writers." A further explanation by the same eulogist, who edited Beaumont's *Original Poems* in 1749, makes all clear. "Our Author," it appears, "did not look upon poetry as the serious business of his life ; for whilst he was thus amusing his leisure hours with the Muses, he wrote a full

and clear commentary upon the Book of Ecclesi-
astes, and large critical notes upon the Pentateuch."
After this, the astonished reader will perhaps be
disinclined to verify the statement, reluctantly
made, that in the poems of our author "we sometimes meet with a vicious copiousness of style, at
others, with an affectation of florid, gay, and
tedious descriptions ; nor did he always use the
language of nature."

Next, Cowley "came in robustiously and put
for it with a deal of violence" in his sacred poem
entitled *Davideis.* In the exordium of the First
Book he proclaims his mission :—

> Too long the *Muses-Lands* have *Heathen* bin
> Their *Gods* too long were *Devils*, and *Vertues Sin ;*
> But *Thou, Eternal World*, hast call'd forth *Me*,
> Th' *Apostle*, to convert that *World* to *Thee ;*
> T' unbind the charms that in slight *Fables* lie,
> And teach that *Truth* is *truest Poesie.*

But it was ·not to be. His "polisht *Pillars* of
strong *Verse*" were destined never to carry a roof.
The theme, so vigorously introduced, soon lan-
guished ; and by the time he had completed a
Fourth Book, it lay, for all his nursing skill,
prematurely dead on his hands. The poem is not
finished, and yet there is nothing to add.

After Cowley in date of composition, but before
him in date of publication, Davenant in his
Gondibert shows traces of the prevalent ambition.

He rejects all supernatural fables, and makes it a point of sound doctrine to choose only Christians for his characters. But that poem, too, broke off in the middle.

In France the question had been as zealously discussed, and had been illustrated by experiments no less elaborate. In 1657, a year after the appearance of Cowley's *Davideis*, Desmarets de Saint-Sorlin brought out his sacred poem of *Clovis*, with a great flourish of trumpets, and a long prose demonstration that its theme was the grandest a French poet could choose. The real supernatural of the Christian religion, so he argued, is a subject much nobler for poetry than the pagan mythology, as the sunlight is brighter than the shadow. The controversy dragged on till 1673, when Boileau, in the third book of his *Poetic*, settled the question for the nonce, and fixed the opinion of the succeeding generation of critics. He casts an equal ridicule upon *Clovis* and upon the theory which it was designed to illustrate :—

> The arts of fiction give the air of lies
> Even to the most unquestioned verities ;
> And what a pious entertainment, too,
> The yells of Satan and his damnèd crew,
> When, proud to assail your Hero's matchless might,
> With God himself they wage a doubtful fight.

So the burial of *Clovis* was hastened by ridicule. Yet every one of the arguments brought against

that poem by Boileau holds equally good against
Paradise Lost, which Milton, knowing as little of
Boileau as Boileau knew of him, had published
some six years earlier. *Paradise Lost*, it might
almost be said, is superior to *Clovis* in nothing,
except the style. By the force of his genius and
the magic of his style, Milton succeeded in an
attempt thought hopeless by the best critical
judges of his century, and won his way through a
ravine that was strewn with the corpses of his epic
predecessors.

His courage and originality are witnessed also
by the metre that he chose for his poem. To us
blank verse seems the natural metre for a long
serious poem. Before Milton's day, except in the
drama, it had only once been so employed—in an
Elizabethan poem of no mark or likelihood, called
A Tale of Two Swannes. While Milton was
writing *Paradise Lost* the critics of his time were
discussing whether the rhymed couplet or some
form of stanza was fitter for narrative poetry, and
whether the couplet or blank verse better suited
the needs of drama. As no one, before Milton,
had maintained in argument that blank verse was
the best English measure for narrative poetry
dealing with lofty themes, so no critic had ever
been at the pains to refute that opinion. In the
year of the publication of *Paradise Lost*, Dryden
delivered his judgment, that the rhymed couplet

was best suited for tragic passages in the drama, and that blank verse should be employed chiefly for the lighter and more colloquial purposes of comedy. Some echo of the courtly dispute then in progress between Dryden and his brother-in-law, Sir Robert Howard, probably reached Milton's ear through his bookseller, Samuel Simmons ; for it was at the request of his bookseller that he added the three Miltonic sentences on "The Verse," by way of preface. With his accustomed confidence and directness of attack he begs the question in his first words :—"The measure is English heroic verse without rime "; and in his closing words he takes credit to himself for his " example set, the first in English, of ancient liberty recovered to heroic poem from the troublesome and modern bondage of riming."

In these two cardinal points, then—the matter and the form of his poem—Milton was original. For the one there was no true precedent in English ; for the other there was no precedent that might not rather have been called a warning. His matter was to be arranged and his verse handled by his own ingenuity and at his own peril. He left a highroad behind him, along which many a tuneful pauper has since limped ; but before him he found nothing but the jungle and false fires. In considering his style, therefore, it is well to treat the problem as it presented itself to him, and to follow his achievement as he won step by step out of the void.

There were two great influences in English poetry, other than the drama, when Milton began to write : the influence of Spenser and the influence of Donne. Only the very slightest traces of either can be discerned in Milton's early verse. There are some Spenserian cadences in the poem *On the Death of a Fair Infant*, written in his seventeenth year :—

> Or wert thou of the golden-wingèd host,
> Who, having clad thyself in human weed,
> To earth from thy prefixèd seat didst post,
> And after short abode fly back with speed,
> As if to show what creatures Heaven doth breed ;
>   Thereby to set the hearts of men on fire
> To scorn the sordid world, and unto Heaven aspire ?

The later verses on *The Passion*, written in the same metre, are perhaps the last in which Milton echoes Spenser, however faintly. Meanwhile, in the hymn *On the Morning of Christ's Nativity*, he had struck a note that was his own, and it is not surprising that he left the poem on the Passion unfinished, "nothing satisfied with what was begun."

As for the great Dean of St. Paul's, there is no evidence that Milton was touched by him, or, for that matter, that he had read any of his poems. In the verses written *At a Vacation Exercise*, he expressly sets aside

> Those new-fangled toys and trimming slight
> Which takes our late fantastics with delight ;

and he very early came to dislike the fashionable conceits that ran riot in contemporary English verse. A certain number of conceits, few and poor enough, is to be found scattered here and there in his early poems. Bleak Winter, for instance, is represented in three cumbrous stanzas, as the slayer of the Fair Infant :—

> For he, being amorous on that lovely dye
> That did thy cheek envermeil, thought to kiss,
> But killed, alas ! and then bewailed his fatal bliss.

In the lines on Shakespeare the monument promised to the dead poet is a marvel of architecture and sculpture, made up of all his readers, frozen to statues by the wonder and astonishment that they feel when they read the plays. But perhaps the nearest approach to a conceit of the metaphysical kind is to be found in that passage of *Comus*, where the Lady accuses Night of having stolen her brothers :—

> O thievish Night,
> Why shouldst thou, but for some felonious end,
> In thy dark lantern thus close up the stars
> Which Nature hung in heaven, and filled their lamps
> With everlasting oil to give due light
> To the misled and lonely traveller ?

When Milton does fall into a vein of conceit, it is generally both trivial and obvious, with none of the saving quality of Donne's remoter extravagances. In Donne they are hardly extravagances; the vast overshadowing canopy of his imagination seems to bring the most wildly dissimilar things together with ease. To his unfettered and questioning thought the real seems unreal, the unreal real; he moves in a world of shadows, cast by the lurid light of his own emotions; they take grotesque shapes and beckon to him, or terrify him. All realities are immaterial and insubstantial; they shift their expressions, and lurk in many forms, leaping forth from the most unlikely disguises, and vanishing as suddenly as they came.

> Sometime we see a cloud that's dragonish;
> A vapour sometime like a bear or lion,
> A tower'd citadel, a pendent rock,
> A forked mountain, or blue promontory
> With trees upon't that nod unto the world,
> And mock our eyes with air : thou hast seen these signs ;
> They are black Vesper's pageants.

They are the poems of John Donne. Nothing could be further from the manner of Milton, or less likely to overcome his own positive imagination. Here are two examples of Donne's best poetic manner :—

> But yet thou canst not die, I know ;
> To leave this world behind, is death ;
> But when thou from this world wilt go,
> The whole world vapours with thy breath.

And again :—

> Twice or thrice had I loved thee,
> Before I knew thy face or name ;
> So in a voice, so in a shapeless flame
> Angels affect us oft, and worshipp'd be.

Let it be considered what Milton means by the terms "World" and "Angel," how clear an external reality each embodies for him. Any forced comparison used by him is not an attempt to express a subtlety, but merely a vicious trick of the intellect. The virtues of the metaphysical school were impossible virtues for one whose mind had no tincture of the metaphysic. Milton, as has been said already, had no deep sense of mystery. One passage of *Il Penseroso*, which might be quoted against this statement, is susceptible of an easier explanation :—

> And if aught else great bards beside
> In sage and solemn tunes have sung,
> Of turneys, and of trophies hung,
> Of forests, and enchantments drear,
> Where more is meant than meets the ear.

He alludes no doubt to Spenser, and by the last line intends only allegory—a definite moral signification affixed to certain characters and stories —not the mystic correspondences that Donne loves. The most mysterious lines in *Comus* are these :—

> A thousand fantasies
> Begin to throng into my memory,
> Of calling shapes, and beckoning shadows dire,
> And airy tongues that syllable men's names
> On sands and shores and desert wildernesses.

They are purely Elizabethan and reminiscent. But if the stranger beauties of the metaphysical school were beyond his reach, its vices touched him wonderfully little, so that his conceits are merely the rare flaws of his early work.

The dramatists were a much more potent influence than either Spenser or the metaphysical school. He learned his blank verse from the dramatists. Perhaps he took the subject of *Comus* from the *Old Wives' Tale* of George Peele ; and when he set himself to write a masque he was doubtless well acquainted with the works of the chief master in that kind, Ben Jonson. William Godwin, in his *Lives of Edward and John Phillips*, expresses the opinion that Milton studied the works of Jonson more assiduously than those of any other Elizabethan. The specific evidence that he cites —a few passages of possible reminiscence—is not convincing. He has no more striking coincidence to show than the resemblance between a phrase in *Il Penseroso* :—

> Come, but keep thy wonted state,

and two lines of Jonson's *Hymn to Cynthia* :—

> Seated in thy silver chair
> State in wonted manner keep.

If the original genius of a poet is to be sworn
away at this rate, there will soon come a time
when no man is secure. Any one who confesses
to "considerable difficulty" in getting upstairs
might hereafter be accused of plagiarism if it
should be found that a Latinist of repute has
stated that "the difficulties of translating Persius
are considerable." Milton doubtless studied
Jonson's works; and, if specific resemblances are
both weighed and counted, a good case can be
made out for the influence of Jonson's prose on
the author of the *Areopagitica*. But the fact is
that criticism finds itself here in a region where
this minute matching of phrase with phrase is
useless or misleading. Milton's early poems grew
on Elizabethan soil, and drank Elizabethan air.
It matters little that there are few verbal coincidences; the influence is omnipresent, easy to
feel, impossible to describe in detail. From whom
but the Elizabethans could he have learned to
write thus ?—

> Fly, envious Time, till thou run out thy race :
> Call on the lazy leaden-stepping Hours,
> Whose speed is but the heavy plummet's pace ;
> And glut thyself with what thy womb devours.

The Elizabethan style is not to be mistaken, the
high-figured phrases, loosely welded together,

lulling the imagination into acquiescence by the flow of the melody. Lines like these might well occur in *Richard II.* The same Shakespearian note is clearly audible in such a passage as this, where Comus describes the two brothers :—

> Their port was more than human, as they stood.
> I took it for a faery vision
> Of some gay creatures of the element,
> That in the colours of the rainbow live,
> And play i' the plighted clouds. I was awe-strook,
> And, as I passed, I worshipped. If those you seek,
> It were a journey like the path to Heaven
> To help you find them.

This has all the technical marks of late Elizabethan dramatic blank verse : " vision " as a trisyllable ; the redundant syllable in the middle of the line ; the colloquial abbreviation of " in the " ; not to mention the fanciful vein of the whole passage, which might lead any one unacquainted with Milton to look for this quotation among the dramas of the prime. The great hyperbolical strain of the Elizabethans, which so often broke into rant, is caught and nobly echoed in praise of virtue :—

> If this fail,
> The pillared firmament is rottenness
> And earth's base built on stubble.

Or, to take a last example of Milton's earlier style, this description of the Lady's singing is in marked contrast to the later matured manner :—

> At last a soft and solemn-breathing sound
> Rose like a steam of rich distilled perfumes,
> And stole upon the air, that even Silence
> Was took ere she was ware, and wished she might
> Deny her nature, and be never more
> Still to be so displaced. I was all ear,
> And took in strains that might create a soul
> Under the ribs of Death.

This has the happy audacity of Shakespeare, and his delight in playing with logic ; it is almost witty. The Miltonic audacity of the later poems is far less diffuse and playful.   When the nightingale sings, in *Paradise Lost*, "Silence was pleased." When Adam begs the Angel to tell the story of the Creation, he adds, "Sleep, listening to thee, will watch."   Either of these paradoxes would have been tormented and elaborated into a puzzle by a true Elizabethan.

Milton, then, began as a pupil of the dramatists. But his tendencies and ambitions were not dramatic, so he escaped the diseases that afflicted the drama in its decadence.   When he began to write blank verse, the blank verse of the dramatists, his contemporaries, was fast degenerating into more or less rhythmical prose.   Suckling and Davenant and their fellows not only used the utmost license of redundant syllables at the end of the line, but hustled and slurred the syllables in the middle till the line was a mere gabble, and interspersed broken lines so plentifully that it became im-

possible even for the most attentive ear to follow
the metre. A brief description of a Puritan
waiting-woman may be taken as an illustration
from Jasper Mayne's comedy of *The City Match*
(1639). As a sample of blank verse it is perhaps
somewhat smoother and more regular than the
average workmanship of that time :—

> She works religious petticoats ; for flowers
> She'll make church-histories. Her needle doth
> So sanctify my cushionets ; besides
> My smock-sleeves have such holy embroideries,
> And are so learned, that I fear in time
> All my apparel will be quoted by
> Some pure instructor. Yesterday I went
> *To see a lady that has a parrot : my woman*
> *While I was in discourse converted the fowl ;*
> And now it can speak nought but Knox's works ;
> So there's a parrot lost.

Blank verse that has learned to tolerate such lines
as the two here set in italics can only end by
becoming prose. And, indeed, that was the
destined development of the drama, even had
the theatres never been closed under the Commonwealth. The history of blank verse reflects with
curious exactness the phases of the history of the
drama. When the metre was first set on the
stage, in the Senecan drama, it was stiff and slow-
moving ; each line was monotonously accented,
and divided from the next by so heavy a stress
that the absence of rhyme seemed a wilful injury

done to the ear. Such as it was, it suited the
solemn moral platitudes that it was called upon to
utter.   Peele, Marlowe, and Shakespeare made
the drama lyrical in theme and treatment; the
measure, adapting itself to the change, became
lyrical in their hands. As the drama grew in
scope and power, addressing itself to a greater
diversity of matter, and coming to closer grips
with the realities of life, the lyrical strain was lost,
and blank verse was stretched and loosened and
made elastic.   During the twenty years of Shakespeare's dramatic activity, from being lyrical it
tended more and more to become conversational
in Comedy, and in Tragedy to depend for its
effects rather on the rhetorical rise and fall of the
period than on the unit of the line.   From the
drama of Charles the First's time, when inferior
workmen had carried these licenses to the verge
of confusion, it is a perfectly natural transition to
the heroic couplet for Tragedy and the well-bred
prose of Etherege for Comedy.   Blank verse had
lost its character; it had to be made vertebrate
to support the modish extravagances of the heroic
plays; and this was done by the addition of
rhyme.   Comedy, on the other hand, was tending
already, long before the civil troubles, to social
satire and the life-like representation of contemporary character and manners, so that prose
was its only effective instrument.

At the time when blank verse was yielding to decay, Milton took it up, and used it neither for conversational nor for rhetorical purposes. In the interests of pure poetry and melody he tightened its joints, stiffened its texture, and one by one gave up almost all the licenses that the dramatists had used. From the first he makes a sparing use of the double ending. The redundant syllable in the middle of the line, which he sometimes allows himself in *Comus*, does not occur in *Paradise Lost*. In the later poem he adopts strict practices with regard to elision, which, with some trifling exceptions, he permits only in the case of contiguous open vowels, and of short unstressed vowels separated by a liquid consonant, in such words, for instance, as "dissolute," or "amorous." By a variety of small observances, which, when fully stated, make up a formidable code, he mended the shambling gait of the loose dramatic blank verse, and made of it a worthy epic metre.

In a long poem variety is indispensable, and he preserved the utmost freedom in some respects. He continually varies the stresses in the line, their number, their weight, and their incidence, letting them fall, when it pleases his ear, on the odd as well as on the even syllables of the line. The pause or cæsura he permits to fall at any place in the line, usually towards the middle, but, on occasion, even after the first or ninth syllables.

His chief study, it will be found, is to vary the word in relation to the foot, and the sentence in relation to the line. No other metre allows of anything like the variety of blank verse in this regard, and no other metrist makes so splendid a use of its freedom. He never forgets the pattern ; yet he never stoops to teach it by the repetition of a monotonous tattoo. Hence there are, perhaps, fewer one-line quotations to be found in the works of Milton than in the works of any other master of blank verse. De Quincey speaks of the "slow planetary wheelings" of Milton's verse, and the metaphor is a happy one ; the verse revolves on its axis at every line, but it always has another motion, and is related to a more distant centre.

It may well be doubted whether Milton could have given a clear exposition of his own prosody. In the only place where he attempts it he finds the elements of musical delight to consist in "apt numbers, fit quantity of syllables, and the sense variously drawn out from one verse into another." By "apt numbers" he probably meant the skilful handling of stress-variation in relation to the sense. But the last of the three is the essential of Miltonic blank verse. There lies the secret for whoso can divine it.

Every well-marked type of blank verse has a natural gait or movement of its own, which it falls into during its ordinary uninspired moods.

Tennyson's blank verse, when it is not carefully guarded and varied, drops into a kind of fluent sing-song. Examples may be taken, almost at random, from the *Idylls of the King*. Here is one :—

> So all the ways were safe from shore to shore,
> But in the heart of Arthur pain was lord.

The elements of musical delight here are almost barbarous in their simplicity. There is a surfeit of assonance—*all, shore, shore, lord ; heart, Arthur ; ways, safe, pain.* The alliteration is without complexity, — a dreary procession of sibilants. Worst of all are the monotonous incidence of the stress, and the unrelieved, undistinguished, crowded poverty of the Saxon monosyllables.

No two such consecutive lines were ever written by Milton. His verse, even in its least admirable passages, does not sing, nor trip with regular alternate stress ; its movement suggests neither dance nor song, but rather the advancing march of a body of troops skilfully handled, with incessant changes in their disposition as they pass over broken ground. He can furnish them with wings when it so pleases him. No analysis of his prosody can explain the wonders of his workmanship. But it is not idle to ask for a close attention to the scansion of lines like these, wherein he describes the upward progress of the Son of God and his escort after the Creation :—

> The heavens and all the constellations rung,
> The planets in their station listening stood,
> While the bright pomp ascended jubilant.

In the last line the first four words marshal the great procession in solid array ; the last two lift it high into the empyrean. Let any one attempt to get the same upward effect with a stress, however light, laid on the last syllable of the line, or with words of fewer than three syllables apiece, and he will have to confess that, however abstruse the rules of its working may be, there is virtue in metrical cunning. The passage in the Seventh Book from which these lines are quoted would justify an entire treatise. The five regular alternate stresses first occur in a line describing the progress over the wide plain of Heaven :—

> He through Heaven,
> That opened wide her blazing portals, led
> To God's eternal house direct the way.

But, indeed, the examination of the music of Milton involves so minute a survey of technical detail as to be tedious to all but a few lovers of theory. The laws of music in verse are very subtle, and, it must be added, very imperfectly ascertained ; so that those who dogmatise on them generally end by slipping into fantasy or pedantry. How carefully and incessantly Milton adjusted the sound to the sense is known to every reader of

Paradise Lost. The dullest ear is caught by the contrast between the opening of the gates of Heaven—

> Heaven opened wide
> Her ever-during gates, harmonious sound
> On golden hinges moving—

and the opening of those other gates—

> On a sudden open fly,
> With impetuous recoil and jarring sound,
> The infernal doors, and on their hinges grate
> Harsh thunder, that the lowest bottom shook
> Of Erebus.

But there are many more delicate instances than these. In the choruses of *Samson Agonistes*, where he reaches the top of his skill, Milton varies even the length of the line. So he has hardly a rule left, save the iambic pattern, which he treats merely as a point of departure or reference, a background or framework to carry the variations imposed upon it by the luxuriance of a perfectly controlled art. The great charm of the metre of Wither, which Charles Lamb admired and imitated, lies in its facile combination of what, for the sake of brevity, may be called the iambic and trochaic movements. In *L'Allegro* and *Il Penseroso* Milton had proved his mastery of both its resources. The gaiety of these lines—

> Haste thee, Nymph, and bring with thee
> Jest, and youthful Jollity—

passes easily into the solemnity of these—

> But let my due feet never fail
> To walk the studious cloister's pale.

In *Samson Agonistes* he sought to extend something of the same liberty to the movement of blank verse. He freely intermixes the falling with the rising stress, shifting the weights from place to place, and often compensating a light patter of syllables in the one half of the line by the introduction of two or three consecutive strong stresses in the other half. Under this treatment the metre of *Gorboduc* breaks into blossom and song :—

> O, how comely it is, and how reviving
> To the spirits of just men long oppressed,
> When God into the hands of their deliverer
> Puts invincible might.

To try to explain this marvel of beauty is to beat the air.

By his deliberate attention to the elements of verbal melody Milton gave a new character to English blank verse. But this is not all. Quite as important is the alteration that he made in the character of English poetic diction.

The essence of the lyric is that it is made up of phrases, not of words. The lines run easily because they run on tracks chosen for their ease by the instinct of generations and worn smooth by use. The lyrical phrase, when the first two or three words of it have been pronounced, finishes itself. From Carew's " Ask me no more," with its long train of imitations, to the latest banality of the music-halls, the songs that catch the ear catch it by the same device. The lyric, that is to say, is almost always dependent for its music on easy idiomatic turns of speech. The surprising word occurs rarely ; with all the greater effect inasmuch as it is embedded in phrases that slip from the tongue without a trace of thought or effort. These phrases naturally allow of little diversity of intonation ; they have the unity of a single word, a single accepted emphasis, and a run of lightly-stressed syllables more or less musical in sequence.

All this Milton changed. He chooses his every word. You cannot guess the adjective from the substantive, nor the end of the phrase from its beginning. He is much given to inverting the natural English order of epithet and noun, that he may gain a greater emphasis for the epithet. His style is not a simple loose-flowing garment, which takes its outline from its natural fall over the figure, but a satin brocade, stiff with gold, exactly fitted to the body. There is substance for it to clothe ; but, as his imitators quickly discovered, it can stand alone. He packs his meaning into the fewest possible words, and studies economy in every trifle. In his later poetry there are no gliding connectives; no polysyllabic conjunctive clauses, which fill the mouth while the brain prepares itself for the next word of value ; no otiose epithets, and very few that court neglect by their familiarity. His poetry is like the eloquence of the Lord Chancellor Bacon, as described by Ben Jonson :—" No man ever spake more neatly, more pressly, more weightily, or suffered less emptiness, less idleness in what he uttered. No member of his speech but consisted of his own graces. His hearers could not cough, or look aside from him, without loss." It is this quality of Milton's verse that makes the exercise of reading it aloud a delight and a trial. Every word is of value. There is no mortar between the stones, each is held in place by the weight of the others, and helps to uphold the building. In reading, every word must be rendered clearly and articulately; to drop one out, or to slur it over, is to take a stone from an arch. Indeed, if Lamb and Hazlitt are right in thinking that Shakespeare's greatest plays cannot be acted, by the same token, Milton's greatest poems cannot be read aloud. For his most sonorous passages the human voice is felt to be too thin an instrument ; the lightest word in the line demands some faint emphasis, so that the strongest could not be raised to its true value unless it were roared through some melodious megaphone.

The carefully jewelled mosaic style was practised very early by Milton. It occurs already in the hymn on the Nativity :—

> See how from far upon the eastern road
> The star-led wizards haste with odours sweet :
> O run, prevent them with thy humble ode
> And lay it lowly at his blessed feet.

The same deliberateness and gentle pause of words one after another rounding and falling like clear drops is found in the song of the Spirit in *Comus* :—

> Sabrina fair,
>   Listen where thou art sitting
> Under the glassy, cool, translucent wave,
>   In twisted braids of lilies knitting
> The loose train of thy amber-dropping hair.

This is the effect which Sir Henry Wotton, Milton's earliest critic, speaks of, in a letter to Milton, as " a certain Doric delicacy in your songs and odes, whereunto I must plainly confess to have seen yet nothing parallel in our language."

There are poems, and good poems among the number, written on a more diffuse principle. If you miss one line you find the idea repeated or persisting in the next. It is quite possible to derive pleasure from the *Faerie Queene* by attending to the leading words, and, for the rest, floating onward on the melody. You can catch the drift with ease. The stream circles in so many eddies that to follow it laboriously throughout its course is felt to be hardly necessary : miss it once and you can often join it again at very near the same point. " But a reader of Milton," as an early critic of Milton remarks, " must be always upon duty ; he is surrounded with sense ; it rises in every line, every word is to the purpose. There are no lazy intervals : all has been considered, and demands and merits observation. Even in the best writers you sometimes find words and sentences which hang on so loosely, you may blow them off. Milton's are all substance and weight : fewer would not have served his turn, and more would have been superfluous. His silence has the same effect, not only that he leaves work for the imagination, when he has entertained it and furnished it with noble materials ; but he expresses himself so concisely, employs words so sparingly, that whoever will possess his ideas must dig for them, and oftentimes pretty far below the surface."

An illustration and contrast may serve to point the moral. Here is an example of Spenser's diffuser style, taken from the second book of the *Faerie Queene*. Guyon, escaped from the cave of Mammon, is guarded, during his swoon, by an angel :—

> Beside his head there satt a faire young man,

(This announces the theme, as in music.)

> Of wondrous beauty and of freshest yeares,

(The fair young man was fair and young.)

> Whose tender bud to blossom new began,

(The fair young man was young.)

> And florish faire above his equal peers.

(The fair young man was fair, fairer even than his
equals, who were also his peers.)

In the remaining lines of the stanza the comparison of his hair to the rays of the sun is played
with in the same way :—

> His snowy front curled with golden heares,
> Like Phœbus' face adorned with sunny rayes,
> Divinely shone ; and two sharp winged sheares,
> Decked with diverse plumes, like painted Jayes,
> Were fixed at his back to cut his ayery wayes.

The whole stanza is beautiful, and musical with the
music of redundance. Nothing could be less like
Milton's mature style. His verse, " with frock of
mail, Adamantean proof," advances proudly and
irresistibly, gaining ground at every step. He
brings a situation before us in two lines, every
word contributing its share :—

> Betwixt these rocky pillars Gabriel sat,
> Chief of the angelic guards, awaiting night.

With as decisive a touch he sketches the story of
Jacob—

> In the field of Luz,
> Dreaming by night under the open sky,
> And waking cried, *This is the gate of Heaven.*

Or the descent of Raphael :—

> Like Maia's son he stood,
> And shook his plumes, that heavenly fragrance filled
> The circuit wide.

The packed line introduced by Milton is of a greater density and conciseness than anything to be found in English literature before it. It is our nearest native counterpart to the force and reserve of the high Virgilian diction. In his *Discourse of the Original and Progress of Satire*, Dryden has called attention to the close-wrought quality of Virgil's work. "Virgil," he says, "could have written sharper satires than either Horace or Juvenal, if he would have employed his talent that way. I will produce a verse and a half of his, in one of his Eclogues, to justify my opinion ; and with commas after every word, to show that he has given almost as many lashes as he has written syllables : it is against a bad poet, whose ill verses be describes :—

> *non tu, in triviis, indocte, solebas*
> *Stridenti, miserum, stipula, disperdere, carmen ?*"
> [Wouldst thou not, blockhead, in the public ways,
> Squander, on scrannel pipe, thy sorry lays ?]

Dryden appreciated the terrible force of this

kind of writing for the purposes of satire. At its best, his own satire attains to something like it, as, for instance, in his description of Shaftesbury's early life :—

> Next this (how wildly will ambition steer),
> A vermin wriggling in the usurper's ear,
> Bartering his venal wit for sums of gold,
> He cast himself into the saint-like mould ;
> Groaned, sighed, and prayed, while godliness was gain,
> The loudest bagpipe of the squeaking train.

Except the first line, which is wholly idle, there is nothing that could be spared here. Pope, also, knew the value of condensation ; but he works in antithetic phrases, so that his single words are less telling ; and where Dryden's lines are swords edged with contempt, Pope's are stings, pointed with spite. Thus, of Lord Hervey :—

> Amphibious thing ! that acting either part,
> The trifling head, or the corrupted heart,
> Fop at the toilet, flatterer at the board,
> Now trips a lady, and now struts a lord.
> Eve's tempter thus the Rabbins have exprest,
> A cherub's face, a reptile all the rest ;
> Beauty that shocks you, parts that none will trust,
> Wit that can creep, and pride that licks the dust.

The necessities of rhyme sometimes hamper both Dryden and Pope ; and the nearest parallel to the manner of Virgil is to be sought in Milton. The famous line describing Samson—

> Eyeless, in Gaza, at the mill, with slaves—

is a good example; the sense of humiliation and
abasement is intensified at every step.   Or, to
take a passage in a very different key of feeling,
the same quality is seen in the description of the
obedience of Eve :—

> Required with gentle sway
> And by her yielded, by him best received,
> Yielded with coy submission, modest pride,
> And sweet, reluctant, amorous delay.

The slight stress and pause needed after each
word, to render the full meaning, produce, when
the words are short as well as emphatic, a line of
terrific weight and impact.   What more heartbreaking effect of weariness and eternity of effort
could be produced in a single line than this, descriptive of the dolorous march of the fallen angels ?—

> O'er many a frozen, many a fiery Alp,
> Rocks, caves, lakes, fens, bogs, dens, and shades of death.

It would be difficult to match this line.   In *The
Tears of Peace*, Chapman has a line (he repeats it
in the *Tragedy of Biron*) which owes some of its
strength to the same cause.   He describes the body
as—

> This glass of air, broken with less than breath,
> This slave, bound face to face to death till death.

The eight stresses give the line a passionate energy.

All superfluous graces are usually discarded by Milton. He steers right onward, and gives the reader no rest. A French critic of that age, who has already been mentioned as the author of *Clovis*, praises Malherbe and Voiture and the worthies of their time, at the expense of the ancients. He calls Homer, especially, " a tattler, who is incessantly repeating the same things in the same idle ridiculous epithets,—*the swift-footed Achilles, the ox-eyed Juno, far-darting Apollo*." Milton felt none of this contempt for Homer, but he discarded the practice. His epithets are chosen to perform one exploit, and are dismissed when it is accomplished. As with single epithets, so with lines and phrases ; he does not employ conventional repetitions either for their lyrical value or for wafting the story on to the next point of interest. He seeks no effects such as Marlowe obtained by the lyrical repetition of the line :—

> To entertain divine Zenocrate.

He arrests the attention at every word ; and when the thing is once said, he has done with it.

In his *Discourse of Satire* Dryden raises an interesting point. He makes mention of "the beautiful turns of words and thoughts, which are as requisite in this, as in heroick poetry itself, of which the satire is undoubtedly a species." His attention, he says, was first called to these by Sir

George Mackenzie, who repeated many of them from Waller and Denham. Thereupon he searched other authors, Cowley, Davenant, and Milton, to find further examples of them; but in vain. At last he had recourse to Spenser, "and there I met with that which I had been looking for so long in vain. Spenser had studied Virgil to as much advantage as Milton had done Homer; and amongst the rest of his excellencies had copied that."

By the "turns of words and thoughts" Dryden here means the repetition of a word or phrase in slightly altered guise as the thought is turned over in the mind and presented in a new aspect. There is an almost epigrammatic neatness about some of the examples that he cites from Ovid and Catullus. It is not surprising that he failed to find these elegant turns in Milton, for they are few. Addison and Steele, writing in the *Tatler*, reproach him with having overlooked the speech of Eve in the Fourth Book of *Paradise Lost*:—

> Sweet is the breath of Morn, her rising sweet,
> With charm of earliest birds; pleasant the Sun,
> When first on this delightful land he spreads
> His orient beams, on herb, tree, fruit, and flower,
> Glistering with dew; fragrant the fertile Earth
> After soft showers; and sweet the coming-on
> Of grateful Evening mild; then silent Night,
> With this her solemn bird, and this fair Moon,
> And these the gems of Heaven, her starry train:

But neither breath of Morn, when she ascends
With charm of earliest birds ; nor rising Sun
On this delightful land ; nor herb, fruit, flower,
Glistering with dew ; nor fragrance after showers
Nor grateful Evening mild ; nor silent Night,
With this her solemn bird, nor walk by moon,
Or glittering star-light, without thee is sweet.

Dryden remarks that the elegance he speaks of is common in Italian sonnets, which are usually written on the turn of the first thought ; and certainly this speech of Eve might be truly compared, in all but the metrical structure, to an interspersed sonnet. There is another elaborate piece of repetition at the close of the Tenth Book, where the humble prostration of Adam and Eve is described in exactly the form of speech used by Adam to propose it. But the repetition in this case is too exact to suit Dryden's meaning ; by a close verbal coincidence the ritual of penitence is emphasised in detail, and the book brought to a restful pause. Scattered here and there throughout Milton's longer poems Dryden might, nevertheless, have found the thing he sought. One instance that he gives is taken from the fourth Georgic of Virgil, where Orpheus, leading Eurydice up from Hell, suddenly turns to look on her :—

> *Cum subita incautum dementia cepit amantem ;*
> *Ignoscenda quidem, scirent si ignoscere Manes.*

This turn—" deserving grace, if grace were known

in Hell"—may easily be matched in Milton. In
the Second Book of *Paradise Lost* is described
how the damned

> feel by turns the bitter change
> Of fierce extremes, extremes by change more fierce.

In the Fifth Book, when Raphael arrives at the
gate of Paradise, the angels

> to his state
> And to his message high in honour rise,
> For on some message high they guessed him bound.

In *Samson Agonistes* it is noted that nations grown
corrupt

> love bondage more than liberty,
> Bondage with ease than strenuous liberty.

Yet in the main Dryden is right, for even
instances like these are not many, and the tricky
neatness of Ovid is nowhere to be found in the
English epic poet.

Milton seldom allows his verse to play in
eddies ; he taxes every line to its fullest capacity,
and wrings the last drop of value from each word.
A signal characteristic of his diction has its origin
in this hard dealing. He is often not satisfied
with one meaning from a word, but will make it
do double duty. Here the Latin element in our
language gave him his opportunity. Words
borrowed from the Latin always change their
usage and value in English air. To the ordinary

intelligence they convey one meaning ; to a scholar's memory they suggest also another. It became the habit of Milton to make use of both values, to assess his words in both capacities. Any page of his work furnishes examples of his delicate care for the original meaning of Latin words, such as *intend*—"intend at home . . . what best may ease the present misery " ; *arrive*—" ere he arrive the happy Isle " ; *obnoxious*—" obnoxious more to all the miseries of life " ; *punctual*—" this opacous Earth, this punctual spot " ; *sagacious*—" sagacious of his quarry from so far " ; *explode* — " the applause they meant turned to exploding hiss " ; *retort*—" with retorted scorn his back he turned " ; *infest*—" find some occasion to infest our foes." The Speaker of the House of Commons had to determine, some years ago, whether it is in order to allude to the Members as "infesting" the House. Had Milton been called upon for such a decision he would doubtless have ruled that the word is applicable only to Members whose deliberate intention is to maim or destroy the constitution of Parliament.

But he was not content to revive the exact classical meaning in place of the vague or weak English acceptation ; he often kept both senses, and loaded the word with two meanings at once. When Samson speaks of Dalila as

That specious monster, my accomplished snare—

P

something of this double sense resides in both epithets. In two words we are told that Dalila was both beautiful and deceitful, that she was skilled in the blandishments of art, and successful in the work of her husband's undoing. With a like double reference Samson calls the secret of his strength "my capital secret." Where light, again, is called the "prime work of God," or where we are told that Hell saw "Heaven ruining from Heaven," the original and derivative senses of the words "prime" and "ruin" are united in the conception. These words, and many others similarly employed, are of Latin origin; but Milton carried his practice over into the Saxon part of our vocabulary. The word "uncouth" is used in a double-barrelled sense in the Second Book of *Paradise Lost*—

> Who shall tempt with wandering feet
> The dark, unbottomed, infinite Abyss,
> And through the palpable obscure find out
> His uncouth way ?

And again in *Samson Agonistes*, where Manoa addresses the Chorus—

> Brethren and men of Dan, for such ye seem,
> Though in this uncouth place.

It was this habit of "verbal curiosity" and condensation which seduced Milton into punning. Some of his puns are very bad. There is a modern idea that a pun is a thing to laugh at. Milton's puns, like Shakespeare's, give no smallest countenance to this theory. Sometimes he plays with what is merely a chance identity of sound, as where Satan, entering Paradise—

> At one slight bound high overleapt all bound.

But in most of these cases it seems likely that he believed in an etymological relation between the two words, and so fancied that he was drawing attention to an original unity of meaning. Some such hypothesis is needful to mitigate the atrocity of his worst pun, in *Paradise Regained*, where he describes

> The ravens with their horny beaks
> Food to Elijah bringing even and morn—
> Though ravenous, taught to abstain from what they brought.

Milton was no philologist, and we may be permitted in charity to suppose that he derived "raven" and "ravenous" from the same root.

Some of his puns are to be justified for another reason—that they are made the weapons of mockery. So when Satan rails against Abdiel he says—

> Thou shalt behold
> Whether by supplication we intend
> Address, and to begirt the Almighty Throne
> Beseeching or besieging.

The long punning-bout between Satan and Belial

in the Sixth Book exemplifies the more usual form of the Miltonic pun. When he introduces the newly-invented artillery, Satan makes a speech, "scoffing in ambiguous words"—

> Ye, who appointed stand,
> Do as you have in charge, and briefly touch
> What we propound, and loud that all may hear.

And again, when it has taken effect, scattering the heavenly host in unseemly disorder, he says—

> If our proposals once again were heard,
> We should compel them to a quick result.

Belial, "in like gamesome mood," replies to the jests of his leader, until, by the providence of Heaven, his wit and his artillery are buried under a weight heavier than themselves. On this whole scene Landor remarks that "the first overt crime of the refractory angels was punning"; and adds, with true Miltonic conciseness, "they fell rapidly after that."

Some minor flaws, which may be found in Milton by those who give a close examination to his works, are to be attributed to the same cause—his love of condensed statement. Mixture of metaphors in poetry is often caused merely by the speed of thought, which presents a subject in a new aspect without care taken to adjust or alter the figure. In these cases the obscurity or violence of expression arises not from defect, but

from excess of thought.   Some few instances occur
in Milton, who, in *Lycidas*, writes thus—

> But now my oat proceeds,
> And listens to the Herald of the Sea.

The syntax of the thought is sufficiently lucid and
orderly, but it is compressed into too few words.
In the Fifth Book of *Paradise Lost* is described
how—

> The Eternal Eye, whose sight discerns
> Abtrusest thoughts, from forth his holy mount,
> And from within the golden lamps that burn
> Nightly before him, saw without their light
> Rebellion rising—saw in whom, how spread
> Among the Sons of Morn, what multitudes
> Were banded to oppose his high decree ;
> And, smiling, to his only Son thus said.

Here, it is true, " the Eternal Eye " smiles and
speaks to his only Son.   But Milton has really
discarded the figure after the words " his high
decree," which bring in a new order of thoughts.
He trusts the reader to follow his thought without
grammatical readjustment — to drop the symbol
and remember only the thing symbolised.   His
trust was warranted, until Landor detected the
solecism.   The clearest case of mixed metaphor ever
charged against Milton occurs in the Eleventh
Book, where the lazar-house is described—

> Sight so deform what heart of rock could long
> Dry-eyed behold ?

Rogers pointed this out to Coleridge, who told Wordsworth that he could not sleep all the next night for thinking of it. What months of insomnia must he not have suffered from the perusal of Shakespeare's works!

The close-wrought style of Milton makes the reading of *Paradise Lost* a hard task in this sense, that it is a severe intellectual exercise, without relaxation. The attention that it demands, word by word, and line by line, could not profitably be given to most books ; so that many readers, trained by a long course of novel-reading to nibble and browse through the pastures of literature, find that Milton yields little or no delight under their treatment, and abandon him in despair.

And yet, with however great reluctance, it must be admitted that the close study and admiring imitation of Milton bring in their train some lesser evils. Meaning may be arranged too compactly in a sentence ; for perfect and ready assimilation some bulk and distention are necessary in language as in diet. Now the study of Milton, if it teaches anything, teaches to discard and abhor all superfluity. He who models himself upon this master will never " go a-begging for some meaning, and labour to be delivered of the great burden of nothing." But he may easily fall into the opposite error of putting " riddles of

wit, by being too scarce of words." He will be
so intent upon the final and perfect expression of
his thought, that his life may pass before he finds
it, and even if, in the end, he should say a thing
well, he is little likely to say it in due season.
" Brevity is attained in matter," says a master of
English prose, " by avoiding idle compliments,
prefaces, protestations, parentheses, superfluous
circuit of figures and digressions : in the composition, by omitting conjunctions—*not only* . . .
*but also, both the one and the other, whereby it cometh
to pass,* and such like idle particles." Either
sort of brevity may be learned from Milton. But
any one who has been compelled to make efforts
of unprompted eloquence, and to choose his expressions while he is on his feet, knows well
how necessary is the function performed by these
same prefaces, protestations, parentheses, and idle
particles. Suavely uttered, they keep expectation
alive in the audience, and give the orator time
to think. Whether in speaking or in writing, no
fluent and popular style can well be without them.
*I should be inclined to say—If I may be permitted
to use the expression—Speaking for myself and for
those who agree with me—It is no great rashness to
assert*—a hundred phrases like these are an indispensable part of an easy writer's, as of an easy
speaker's, equipment. To forego all these swollen
and diluted forms of speech is to run the risk of

the opposite danger, congestion of the thought and paralysis of the pen — the scholar's melancholy. To give long days and nights to the study of Milton is to cultivate the critical faculty to so high a pitch that it may possibly become tyrannical, and learn to distaste all free writing. Accustomed to control and punish wanton activity, it will anticipate its judicial duties, and, not content with inflicting death, will devote its malign energy to preventing birth.

It is good, therefore, to remember that Milton himself took a holiday sometimes, and gave a loose to his pen and to his thought. Some parts of his prose writings run in a full torrent of un-chastened eloquence. An open playground for exuberant activity is of the first importance for a writer. Johnson found such a playground in talk. There he could take the curb off his prejudices, give the rein to his whimsical fancy, and better his expression as he talked. But where men must talk, as well as write, upon oath, paralysis is not easily avoided. In the little mincing societies addicted to intellectual and moral culture the creative zest is lost. The painful inhibition of a continual rigorous choice, if it is never relaxed, cripples the activity of the mind. Those who can talk the best and most compact sense have often found irresponsible paradox and nonsense a useful and pleasant

recreation ground. It was Milton's misfortune,
not the least of those put upon him by the bad
age in which he lived, that what Shakespeare
found in the tavern he had to seek in the Church.
Denied the wild wit-combats of the Mermaid, he
disported himself in a pamphlet-war on bishops
and divorce. But he found health and exercise
for his faculties there ; and the moral (for all
things have a moral) is this : that when, in a
mood of self-indulgence, we can write habitually
with the gust, the licentious force, the flow, and
the careless wealthy insolence of the *Animadver-
sions upon the Remonstrant's Defence against Smectymnuus*, we need not then repine or be ill-content
if we find that we can rise only occasionally to the
chastity, the severity, and the girded majesty of
Paradise Lost.

CHAPTER VI

THE STYLE OF MILTON; AND ITS INFLUENCE
ON ENGLISH POETRY

WHEN Milton was born, Shakespeare, Jonson,
Beaumont, Dekker, Chapman, Daniel, Drayton,
and half a hundred other Elizabethan notables
were yet alive. When he died, Addison, Swift,
Steele, and Arbuthnot were already born. Thus
his life bridges the gulf between the age of Elizabeth and the age of Anne; and this further
examination of his style has for object to inquire
what part he may claim in the change of temper,
method, subject, and form which came over
English poetry during that period.

The answer usually given to this question is
that he had no part at all. He lived and died
alone. He imitated no one, and founded no
school. There was none of his more distinguished
contemporaries with whom he was on terms of
intimacy; none whose ideals in poetry remotely
resembled his. So that although he is to be

ranged among the greatest of English poets, a place in the legitimate hereditary succession would, on these considerations, be denied to him. When Dryden succeeded to the dictatorship of Jonson, the continuity of literary history was resumed. The great processes of change which affected English letters during the seventeenth century are in no way associated with the name of Milton. Waller and Denham, Davenant and Dryden, " reformed " English verse ; Hobbes, Cowley, Tillotson, Dryden and Sprat remodelled English prose. And in the meantime, if this account is to be accepted, while English verse and English prose were in the melting-pot, this splendid efflorescence was an accident, a by-product, without meaning or causal virtue in the chemical process that was going forward.

Others will have it that Milton was a belated Elizabethan. But the difficulty of that theory is that he reversed rather than continued many of the practices of the Elizabethans, and introduced reforms of his own, no less striking than the reforms effected by Dryden. Shirley is a good example of a genuine late Elizabethan. But in Shirley's works there is nothing that is not an echo. In Milton's, on the other hand, after the volume of 1645, there is nothing that echoes any earlier English poet even faintly. He renayed his ancestry ; and, if he left no descendants, he must needs be regarded as "a vast species alone."

The Elizabethans, including even the author of *Sejanus* and the translator of Homer, were Romantics. The terms Romantic and Classic are perhaps something overworn; and, although they are useful to supply a reason, it may well be doubted whether they ever helped any one to an understanding. Yet here, if anywhere, they are in place; for Milton is, by common consent, not only a Classic poet, but the greatest exemplar of the style in the long bead-roll of English poets. The "Augustans" prided themselves on their resemblance to the poets of the great age of Rome. Was there nothing in common between them and Milton, and did they really borrow nothing and learn nothing from him?

This much is agreed, that of all English styles Milton's is best entitled to the name of Classic. In his poems may be found every device that belongs to the Classic manner, as in Shakespeare's plays may be found every device that belongs distinctively to the Romantic. Perhaps the two manners are best compared by the juxtaposition of descriptive passages. In description it is impossible for literature to be exhaustive; a choice must be made, an aspect emphasised, and by far the greater part left to the imagination of the reader. A man, for instance, has stature, feature, bones, muscles,

nerves, entrails ; his eyes, hair, and skin are of
certain colours ; he stands in a particular attitude
at a particular spot on the surface of the earth ;
he is agitated by certain passions and ideas; every
movement that he makes is related to his constitution and his past history ; he has affinity with
other men by the ties of the family, the society,
the State ; he thinks and acts more in a minute
than a hundred writers can describe and explain in
a year ; he is a laughing, weeping, money-making,
clothes-wearing, lying, reasoning, worshipping,
amorous, credulous, sceptical, imitative, combative,
gregarious, prehensile, two-legged animal. He
does not cease to be all this and more, merely
because he happens to be at one of his thousand
tricks, and you catch him in the act. How do
you propose to describe him ?

Broadly speaking, there are two methods avail-
able. You may begin with the more general and
comprehensive of the relations that fall in with
your purpose, securing breadth of view and truth
in the larger values, leaving the imagination to
supply the more particular and personal details on
the barest of hints from you : or you may fix your
gaze exclusively on some vivid cluster of details,
indicating their remoter relations and their place
in a wider perspective by a few vague suggestions.

The first of these ways is Milton's. He maps
out his descriptions in bold outline, attending

always to the unity of the picture and the truth of the larger relations. He is chary of detail, and what he adds is added for its own immediate importance rather than for its remoter power of suggestion. Adam and Eve when they are first introduced, are thus described :—

> Two of far nobler shape, erect and tall,
> Godlike erect, with native honour clad
> In naked majesty, seemed lords of all,
> And worthy seemed ; for in their looks divine
> The image of their glorious Maker shone,
> Truth, wisdom, sanctitude severe and pure,—
> Severe, but in true filial freedom placed,
> Whence true authority in men.

As pictorial description this is all but completely empty. It tells you only that they stood upright, that they were like their Maker, and that they were possessed of the virtues that their appearance would lead you to expect. Their physical delineation is to be accommodated by the imagination of the reader to this long catalogue of moral qualities, —nobility, honour, majesty, lordliness, worth, divinity, glory, brightness, truth, wisdom, sanctitude, severity, and purity. In the following lines the poet proceeds to distinguish the one figure from the other, adding a few details with regard to each. The epithets he chooses are still vague. Adam's forehead is " fair " and " large," his eye is " sublime," his locks are " hyacinthine," and (a

detail that has escaped the notice of many illustra-
tors of *Paradise Lost*) they fall in clusters as low
as his shoulders. From beginning to end of the
description the aim of the poet is to preserve the
right key of large emotion, and the words that he
chooses are chosen chiefly for their emotional
value. The emotions are given ; the portraiture
is left to be filled in by the imagination.

Shakespeare commonly works in the reverse
way. He does not, like Crabbe, describe " as if
for the police " ; he chooses his detail with consummate skill, but he makes use of it to suggest
the emotions. It is impossible to set his description of persons over against Milton's ; for the
drama does not describe persons, it presents them
in action ; and a description, where it occurs, is
often designed merely to throw light on the character and feelings of the speaker. " Her voice
was ever soft, gentle, and low " is a description
rather of Lear, as he hangs over the dead body of
Cordelia, refusing to believe that she is dead, than
of Cordelia herself. " An excellent thing in
woman " is not a doctrine, but a last heartbreaking
movement of defiance, as if to refute any stander-
by who dares to think that there is something
amiss, that a voice should not be so low as to be
inaudible.

The contrast of the methods may, therefore, be
better noted in the description of scenes. There

is no very close parallel obtainable ; but the two passages compared by Lessing are not wholly dissimilar in theme, and serve well enough to illustrate the difference of the styles. The first, taken from the Seventh Book of *Paradise Lost*, tells how the King of Glory, from the verge of his heavenly domain, beholds the gulf of Chaos :—

> On Heavenly ground they stood, and from the shore
> They viewed the vast immeasurable Abyss,
> Outrageous as a sea, dark, wasteful, wild,
> Up from the bottom turned by furious winds
> And surging waves, as mountains to assault
> Heaven's highth, and with the centre mix the pole.

The other is the imaginary view from Dover Cliff, described by Edgar in *King Lear :*—

> How fearful
> And dizzy 'tis, to cast one's eyes so low !
> The crows and choughs that wing the midway air
> Show scarce so gross as beetles : half way down
> Hangs one that gathers samphire, dreadful trade !
> Methinks he seems no bigger than his head ;
> The fishermen, that walk upon the beach,
> Appear like mice ; and yond tall anchoring bark,
> Diminish'd to her cock ; her cock, a buoy
> Almost too small for sight : the murmuring surge
> That on th' unnumbered idle pebbles chafes,
> Cannot be heard so high. I'll look no more ;
> Lest my brain turn and the deficient sight
> Topple down headlong.

Johnson objected to this description : " No, sir ; it should be all precipice,—all vacuum.

The crows impede your fall. The diminished appearance of the boats, and other circumstances, are all very good description, but do not impress the mind at once with the horrible idea of immense height. The impression is divided ; you pass on, by computation, from one stage of the tremendous space to another."

This criticism is, in effect, a plea for Milton's method, although by a freak of fate it was uttered in vindication of Congreve. Some years earlier, in his edition of Shakespeare, Johnson had re- marked on the same passage, and had indicated the poetic method that he approved : " He that looks from a precipice finds himself assailed by one great and dreadful image of irresistible de- struction."

Johnson's critical opinions on poetry are deserv- ing of the most careful consideration, and, where they fail to convince, of an undiminished respect. But not Johnson himself can raise a doubt as to which of the two passages quoted above is the greater masterpiece of description proper. Shake- speare sets a scene before your eyes, and by his happy choice of vivid impression makes you giddy. The crows help, rather than impede your fall; for to look into illimitable vacuum is to look at nothing, and therefore to be unmoved. But the classic manner is so careful for unity of emotional impression that it rejects these humble means for

attaining even to so great an end. It refuses to
work by mice and beetles, lest the sudden intrusion
of trivial associations should mar the main impression. No sharp discords are allowed, even though
they should be resolved the moment after. Every
word and every image must help forward the main
purpose. Thus, while the besetting sin of the
Romantics is the employment of excessive, or irrelevant, or trivial or grotesque detail, the besetting
sin of the Classics is so complete an absence of
realistic detail that the description becomes inflated,
windy and empty, and the strongest words in the
language lose their vital force because they are set
fluttering hither and thither in multitudes, with no
substantial hold upon reality. There is nothing
that dies sooner than an emotion when it is cut off
from the stock on which it grows. The descriptive epithet or adjective, if only it be sparingly
and skilfully employed, so that the substantive
carry it easily, is the strongest word in a sentence.
But when once it loses its hold upon concrete
reality it becomes the weakest, and not all the
protests of debility, superlative degrees, and rhetorical insistence, can save it from neglect.

It is apparent, therefore, how necessary to
Milton were the concrete epic realities with which
his poem deals,—the topographical scheme of
things, and the definite embodiment of all his
spiritual essences. Keats' *Hyperion* fails largely

for want of an exact physical system such as
Milton devises. Keats works almost wholly with
vague Romantic suggestion, and there is nothing
for the poem to hang on by. Something is happening ; but it is difficult to say what, for we see
only dream-imagery, and hear only muffled echoes.
Had Milton made unsparing use of abstraction
and suggestion, his poem would have fallen into
windy chaos. The " philosophical poems " of his
age did so fall. Henry More's *Platonick Song
of the Soul* (1642), wherein are treated the Life
of the Soul, her Immortality, the Sleep of the
Soul, the Unity of Souls, and Memory after
Death, is a dust-storm of verbiage. Such words
as " calefaction," " exility," " self-reduplication,"
" tricentreity," " individuation," " circumvolu-
tion," " presentifick circularity," struggle and
sprawl within the narrow room of the Spenserian
stanza. Milton keeps us in better company than
this, even in Hell. He uses abstract terms magnificently, but almost always with a reference to
concrete realities, not as the names of separate
entities. By the substitution of abstract nouns for
concrete he achieves a wonderful effect of majesty.
He does not name, for instance, the particular
form of wind instrument that the heralds blew in
Hell :—

> Four speedy Cherubim
> Put to their mouths the sounding alchymy.

He avoids defining his creatures by names that lend themselves to definite picture : of Death he says—

> So spake the grisly Terror ;

and he makes Raphael, at the call of Heaven's king, rise

> from among
> Thousand celestial Ardours.

In the Tenth Book, Death, snuffing the distant scent of mortality, becomes all nose—

> So scented the grim Feature, and upturned
> His nostril wide into the murky air.

A superb example of this powerful use of abstract terms is contained in the First Book of *Paradise Regained*, where is described how Satan, disguised as an old man, took his leave of the Son of God, and

> Bowing low
> His gray dissimulation, disappeared
> Into thin air diffused.

The word "dissimulation" expresses the fact of the gray hairs assumed, the purpose of deceit, the cringing attitude, and adds a vague effect of power. The same vagueness is habitually studied by Milton in such phrases as "the vast abrupt," "the palpable obscure," "the void immense," "the wasteful deep," where, by the use of an adjective

in place of a substantive, the danger of a definite
and inadequate conception is avoided.

Milton, therefore, describes the concrete, the
specific, the individual, using general and abstract
terms for the sake of the dignity and scope that
they lend. The best of our Romantic poets follow
the opposite course: they are much concerned with
abstract conceptions and general truths, but they
bring them home by the employment of concrete
and specific terms, and figures so familiar that they
cannot easily avoid grotesque associations. These
grotesque associations, however trivial, are the
delight of humour : Alexander's dust will stop
a beer-barrel ; divine ambition exposes

> what is mortal and unsure
> To all that fortune, death, and danger dare,
> Even for an egg-shell.

The comments made by Johnson on a certain
well-known passage in *Macbeth* are an excellent
example of the objections urged against the
Romantic method—a method whereby, says Johnson, poetry is " debased by mean expressions."
He takes for text the invocation of Night by Lady
Macbeth—

> Come, thick night,
> And pall thee in the dunnest smoke of hell,
> That my keen knife see not the wound it makes,
> Nor heaven peep through the blanket of the dark,
> To cry, "Hold, hold!"

Johnson's criticisms, which take up a whole paper in *The Rambler*, may be conveniently stated in summary. The epithet *dun*, he says, is "an epithet now seldom heard but in the stable, and *dun* night may come and go without any other notice but contempt." A *knife*, again, is "an instrument used by butchers and cooks in the meanest employments ; we do not immediately conceive that any crime of importance is to be committed with a *knife*." In the third place, although to wish to elude the eye of Providence is "the utmost extravagance of determined wickedness," yet even this great conception is debased by two unfortunate words when the avengers of guilt are made to *peep* through a *blanket*.

It is easy, in this case at least, to defend Shakespeare. There is no need to make much of the fact that Johnson attributes the speech to Macbeth. The essence of the crime is that it is the treacherous and cowardly crime of an assassin, committed on a guest while he sleeps. Implements of war are out of place here ; it is the very crime for a knife, and Lady Macbeth shows her sense of this when she uses the word. Again, the darkness that she invokes is not the solemn shadow of night, but the stifling, opaque smoke of Hell. The blanket was perhaps suggested to Shakespeare by the black canopy that hung over the Elizabethan stage to represent night ; but, in any case, it gives the notion of an artificial privacy, shutting out light and shutting in sound, a smothered unnatural secrecy. The use of the word *blanket*, in fact, carries with it a new fantastic horror. Night herself, who has brought the fatal gift of sleep to Duncan, is represented as the cowardly accomplice of the murderers, performing the most dastardly office that can fall to the hireling of a bravo.

The mean associations, therefore, in so far as they exist, help Shakespeare's purpose. Milton had no purpose that could be furthered by such help. The omissions in his descriptions cannot be supplied by an appeal to experience, for what he describes is outside the pale of human experience, and is, in that sense, unreal. His descriptions do not so much remind us of what we have seen as create for us what we are to see. He is bound, therefore, to avoid the slightest touch of unworthy association ; the use of even a few domestic figures and homely phrases would bring his hanging palace about his ears. What dangers he escaped may be well seen in Cowley's *Davideis*, which fell into them all. This is how Cowley describes the attiring of his Gabriel, who is commissioned to bear a message to David—

> He took for skin a cloud most soft and bright,
> That e'er the midday Sun pierced through with light :
> Upon his cheeks a lively blush he spred ;
> Washt from the morning beauties deepest red.

> An harmless flaming *Meteor* shone for haire,
> And fell adown his shoulders with loose care.
> He cuts out a silk *Mantle* from the skies,
> Where the most sprightly azure pleas'd the eyes.
> This he with starry vapours spangles all,
> Took in their prime ere they grow *ripe* and *fall*,—

—and so on. The whole business suggests the arming of Pigwiggin ; or the intricacies of Belinda's toilet in *The Rape of the Lock*. Such a Gabriel should add the last touch of adornment from a patch-box filled with sun-spots ; and then is fit only to be—

> Drawn with a team of little atomies
> Athwart men's noses as they lie asleep.

Milton was not in the least likely to fall into this fantastic-familiar vein. But he was also debarred from dealing freely in realism ; from carrying conviction by some sudden startling piece of fidelity to the mixed texture of human experience and human feeling. When the feast is spread in Eden he remarks, it is true,—" No fear lest dinner cool " ; but a lapse like this is of the rarest. His success—and he knew it—depended on the untiring maintenance of a superhuman elevation. His choice of subject had therefore not a little to do with the nature of his diction ; and, through the influence of his diction, as shall be shown hereafter, with the establishment of the poetic tradition that dominated Eighteenth Century poetry.

The same motives and tendencies, the same consistent care for remoteness and loftiness, may be seen in the character of the similes that he most frequently employs. Almost all his figures and comparisons illustrate concrete objects by concrete objects, and occurrences in time by other occurrences later in time. The essentially Romantic sort of figure, scarcely used by Milton, illustrates subtle conceptual relations by parable—

> Now at the last gasp of Love's latest breath,
> When, his pulse failing, Passion speechless lies,
> And Faith is kneeling by his bed of death,
> And Innocence is closing up his eyes,—
> Now, if thou would'st, when all have given him over,
> From death to life thou might'st him yet recover.

Sometimes. by a curious reversal, poets, especially the more sophisticated poets of the Romantic Revival, describe a perfectly definite outward object or scene by a figure drawn from the most complex abstract conceptions. So Shelley, with whom these inverted figures are habitual, compares the skylark to

> A poet hidden
> In the light of thought ;

and Byron, describing the rainbow over a waterfall, likens it to

> Love watching Madness with unalterable mien.

Both ways are foreign to the epic manner of Milton. His figures may be called historic parallels, whereby the names and incidents of human history are made to elucidate and ennoble the less familiar names and incidents of his pre-historic theme. Sometimes, following Homer, he borrows a figure from rustic life, as where, for instance, he compares the devils, crowding into Pandemonium, to a swarm of bees. But he per-ceived clearly enough that he could not, for the reasons already explained, afford to deal largely in this class of figure : he prefers to maintain dignity and distance by choosing comparisons from ancient history and mythology, or from those great and strange things in Nature which repel intimacy— the sun, the moon, the sea, planets in opposition, a shooting star, an evening mist, a will-o'-the-wisp, a vulture descending from the Himalayas, the ice-floes on the North-East passage, the sea-beast leviathan, Xerxes' Hellespontic bridge, the gryphon pursuing the Arimaspian, the madness of Alcides in Oeta, the rape of Proserpine, and a hundred more reminiscences of the ancient world.

Even the great events of ancient history seemed to him at times too familiar, too little elevated and remote to furnish a resting-place for a song that intended "no middle flight." He transforms his proper names, both to make them more melodious, and to make them more unfamiliar to the ear.

No praise is too high for his art and skill in this
matter. An example may be found in those four
lines—the earliest that have the full Miltonic
resonance—describing the fate of Lycidas, carried
by the tide southward to the Cornish coast :—

> Or whether thou, to our moist vows denied,
> Sleep'st by the fable of Bellerus old,
> Where the great Vision of the guarded mount
> Looks toward Namancos and Bayona's hold.

" Bellerus " seems to be a name of Milton's
coinage. He had written " Corineus," and
probably disliked the sound, for in this case it can
hardly have been that the name was too familiar.
Both reasons concurred in prompting the allusion
to Pharaoh and his Egyptian squadrons as—

> Busiris and his Memphian chivalry.

One would think "Italy" a pleasant enough sound,
and " Vulcan " a good enough name for poetry.
Neither was musical enough for Milton ; both
perhaps had associations too numerous, familiar,
and misleading. Vulcan is mentioned, by that
name, in *Comus ;* but in *Paradise Lost*, where the
story of his fall from Heaven is told, and the
architect of Pandemonium is identified with him,
both names, "Italy" and " Vulcan," are heightened
and improved :—

> In Ausonian land
> Men called him Mulciber.

"Hephaistos," the name dear to moderns, could have found no place in Milton's works, unless it had been put in a description of the God's smithy, or, perhaps, in the sonnet where are pilloried those harsh-sounding Presbyterian names :—

Colkitto, or Macdonnel, or Galasp.

Milton's use of proper names is a measure of his poetic genius. He does not forego it even in the lyric. Was there ever so learned a lyric as that beginning "Sabrina fair"—with its rich stores of marine mythology ? History, not philosophy, was the source that he drew on for his splendours ; and history, according to Milton, had, since the Fall of Man, furnished nothing but fainter and weaker repetitions of those stupendous events which filled the early theatre of universal space.

His epic catalogues, which are few in number, show the same predominant interest in history and geography. The story of the Creation gave him an excellent opportunity of enumerating the kinds and properties of birds, beasts, fishes, and reptiles, plants and trees, after the manner of Chaucer and Spenser. This opportunity he refuses, or, at any rate, turns to but small account. His general descriptions are highly picturesque, but he spends little time on enumeration and detail. Of vegetables, only the vine, the gourd, and the corn are mentioned by name ; of the inhabitants of the sea only the seal, the dolphin, and the whale. Natural knowledge, although he made a fair place for it in his scheme of education, was not one of his dearer studies. It was enough for him, as for Raphael that Adam knew the natures of the beasts, and gave them appropriate names. The mere mention, on the other hand, of historic and geographic names rouses all the poet in him. The splendid roll-call of the devils, in the First Book of *Paradise Lost*, and the only less splendid enumeration, in the Eleventh Book, of the Kingdoms of the Earth, shown to Adam in vision, are a standing testimony to his powers. Compared with these, the list of human diseases and maladies in the Eleventh Book, suggested perhaps by Du Bartas, is rehearsed in a slighter and more perfunctory fashion.

One last point in Milton's treatment must not be left unnoticed. Much adverse criticism has been spent on his allegorical figures of Sin and Death. There is good classical precedent for the introduction of such personified abstractions among the actors of a drama ; and, seeing that the introduction of sin and death into the world was the chief effect of his main action, Milton no doubt felt that this too must be handled in right epic fashion, and must not be left to be added to the theme as a kind of embroidery of moral philosophy. In no other way could he have treated the topic half so effectively. There is enough of his philosophy in Milton's Heaven to damp our desire for more of it on his Earth or in his Hell. And when once we have given him license to deal only in persons, we are amply rewarded. His management of the poetic figure of personification is superb. It is a figure difficult to handle, and generally fails of effect through falling into one of two extremes. Either the quality, or the person, is forgotten. The figures in the *Romaunt of the Rose* are good examples of the one type, of the minute materialistic personifications of the Middle Ages, pictorial rather than literary in essence, like the illuminated figures in a psalter. The feeble abstractions that people Gray's Odes, where, as Coleridge remarked, the personification depends wholly on the use of an initial capital, are examples of the other. Neither has the art of combining the vastness and vagueness of the abstract with the precise and definite conception of a person, as is done in the great figure of Religion drawn by Lucretius, as is done also in those other figures— the only creations of English poetry which approach the Latin in grandeur—the horrible phantoms of Sin and Death.

These, then, here outlined slightly and imperfectly, are some of the most noteworthy features of Milton's style. By the measured roll of his verse, and the artful distribution of stress and pause

to avoid monotony and to lift the successive lines
in a climax ; by the deliberate and choice character
of his diction, and his wealth of vaguely emotional
epithets ; by the intuition which taught him to use
no figures that do not heighten the majesty, and
no names that do not help the music of his poem ;
by the vivid outlines of the concrete imaginations
that he imposes on us for real, and the cloudy
brilliance that he weaves for them out of all great
historical memories, and all far-reaching abstract
conceptions, he attained to a finished style of
perhaps a more consistent and unflagging elevation
than is to be found elsewhere in literature.   There
is nothing to put beside him.   " His natural port,"
says Johnson, " is gigantick loftiness."   And
Landor : " After I have been reading the *Paradise
Lost*, I can take up no other poet with satisfaction.
I seem to have left the music of Handel for the
music of the streets, or, at best, for drums and
fifes."   The secret of the style is lost ; and no
poet, since Milton's day, has recaptured the
solemnity and beauty of the large utterance of
Gabriel, or Belial, or Satan.

The success of *Paradise Lost*, when it was
published in 1667, was immediate and startling.
Some of the poet's biographers have shed tears
over the ten pounds that was all Milton ever
received for his greatest work ; others, mag-

nanimously renouncing the world on his behalf, have rejoiced in the smallness of the sum paid him for a priceless work. Lament and heroics are both out of place. London was a small town, and it may well be doubted whether any modern provincial town of the same size would buy up in eighteen months thirteen hundred copies of a poem so serious and difficult and novel as *Paradise Lost*. Moreover, before the close of the century, six editions had appeared, three of them in folio, and so—judged by the number of editions—Milton's epic had outrun Shakespeare's plays in popularity. The folio edition of 1695, with notes and elucidations by one Patrick Hume, a Scottish scholar, appeared fourteen years before Nicholas Rowe produced the first critical edition of Shakespeare. The literary world quickly came to the opinion expressed by Dryden in the year of Milton's death, that the *Paradise Lost* was "one of the greatest, most noble, and most sublime poems which either this age or nation has produced." Barely twenty years later the editors of the *Athenian Mercury* were asked to determine "Whether Milton and Waller were not the best English Poets; and which the better of the two?" Their verdict, reflecting, no doubt, the average opinion of the time, ran thus: "They were both excellent in their kind, and exceeded each other, and all besides. Milton was the fullest and loftiest ; Waller the neatest and most correct poet we ever had." Long before Addison wrote the papers on *Paradise Lost* in the *Spectator*, Milton had received full recognition in the literary handbooks of that age. Langbaine, in his *Account of the English Dramatick Poets* (1691), takes notice of Dryden's debts to *Samson Agonistes*, and, with an effort to be just, remarks of Milton :—" Had his Principles been as good as his Parts, he had been an Excellent Person." Sir Thomas Pope Blount, in his *De Re Poetica* (1694), and Bysshe in his *Art of English Poetry* (1702), bear witness, in their several ways, to Milton's great and assured fame. Indeed, Thomas Rymer, of Gray's Inn, Esquire, who in 1677 had sneered at "that *Paradise Lost* of Milton's which some are pleased to call a Poem," and William Winstanley, who, in the *Lives of the Most Famous English Poets* (1687), had remarked of Milton that "his Fame is gone out like a Candle in a Snuff, and his Memory will always stink," were almost alone among the voices of their time. They were still under the influence of the old political prejudice, but they did battle for a doomed opinion, and, among judges not illiterate, they are the poet's last detractors.

The singular thing to note is that the eighteenth century, which broke with almost every other seventeenth-century poet before Dryden, did not

R

break with Milton. "Who now reads Cowley?"
Pope asked : Cowley, whose works ran through so
many editions that no modern reprint has been
called for. If he had asked, "Who now reads
Milton?" the answer must have been, "Every
writer of English verse"; and so it has continued
from the time of Milton's death to the present
day. The choice of blank verse for *Paradise
Lost* established that metre in formidable rivalry
to the heroic couplet, so that it became the usual
metre for long poems of a reflective or descriptive
cast. Professed imitations of Milton's verse were
many ; among them, Addison's *Translation of a
Story out of the Third Aeneid*, Broome's experi-
ment in the translation of the Eleventh Odyssey,
Fenton's fragments of two books of the *Iliad*,
and Christopher Pitt's paraphrase of Psalm cxxxix.
In the first year of the eighteenth century John
Philips showed, in his *Splendid Shilling*, how the
style of Milton might be applied, for the purposes
of burlesque, to humble subjects, a lesson which
he further illustrated, with no ostensible comic
intent, in his later poems, *Cyder* and *Blenheim*.
Gay, in *Wine, a Poem*, Somerville in *The Chase*,
Armstrong in *The Oeconomy of Love* and *The Art
of Preserving Health*, Christopher Smart in *The
Hop-Garden*, Dyer in *The Fleece*, and Grainger in
The Sugar-Cane, all followed where Philips' *Cyder*
had led, and multiplied year by year what may

be called the technical and industrial applications
of Milton's style.   Among the many other blank
verse poems produced during the middle part of
the century it is enough to name Thomson's
Seasons; Blair's *Grave*; Glover's *Leonidas*; Shen-
stone's *Economy*, *The Ruined Abbey*, and *Love and
Honour*; Young's *Night Thoughts*; Akenside's
Pleasures of the Imagination; Thomas Warton's
Pleasures of Melancholy; Mallet's *The Excursion*,
and *Amyntor and Theodora*; Cooper's *The Power
of Harmony*; and Lyttelton's *Blenheim*.   The
influence of Milton is not equally apparent in all
of these, but in none is it wholly wanting ; in most
it is visible on every page.   The mere invocation
often tells a tale.   Thus Akenside :—

> Thou chief, Poetic Spirit, from the banks
> Of Avon, whence thy holy fingers cull
> Fresh flowers and dews to sprinkle on the turf
> Where Shakespeare lies, be present.   And with thee
> Let Fiction come ; on her aërial wings
> Wafting ten thousand colours.

The quotation need not be prolonged ; even while
he commemorates Shakespeare, Akenside goes to
Milton for his material, and plays a feeble variation
on the Miltonic phrase :—

> In his right hand
> Grasping ten thousand thunders.

Thus Lyttelton :—

> Minerva, thee to my adventurous lyre
> Assistant I invoke, that means to sing
> Blenheim, proud monument of British fame
> Thy glorious work !

" The building, not the field, I sing," he might
have added, for Philips had already chanted the
battle of Blenheim in like Miltonic fashion.
Thus, again, the worthy Grainger, flattest of
agricultural bards :—

> Spirit of Inspiration, that did'st lead
> Th' Ascrean poet to the sacred mount,
> And taught'st him all the precepts of the swain ;
> Descend from Heaven, and guide my trembling steps
> To Fame's eternal dome, where Maro reigns ;
> Where pastoral Dyer, where Pomona's bard,
> And Smart and Somervile in varying strains,
> Their sylvan lore convey : O may I join
> This choral band, and from their precepts learn
> To deck my theme, which though to song unknown,
> Is most momentous to my country's weal !

Grainger frequently echoes Milton ; and in the
passage where he addresses the Avon, at Bristol,
he pays a more explicit tribute :—

> Though not to you, young Shakespeare, Fancy's child,
> All-rudely warbled his first woodland notes ;
>   *   *   *   *   *   *
> On you reclined, another tuned his pipe ,
> Whom all the Muses emulously love,
> And in whose strains your praises shall endure
> While to Sabrina spreads your healing stream.

Better and more striking instances of the Miltonic spell laid on blank verse are easily to be found for the seeking. But since it is the omnipresence of this Miltonic influence that is asserted, passages like these, which catch the eye on any chance page of eighteenth-century blank verse, and are representative of hundreds more, suffice for the purpose.

There has been a tendency among recent historians of English literature to group together the poets who, like Dyer in *Grongar Hill*, and Thomas Warton in *The Pleasures of Melancholy*, echo the strains of Milton's early poems, and to name them "Miltonics," precursors of the Romantic Revival. No doubt there is a marked difference between Milton's earlier manner and his later ; not a few of his lovers, if they were forced to choose, would readily give up the three major poems to save the five best of the minor. But it is going far to appropriate the name of "Miltonic" to imitators of the earlier poems. Perhaps the study of *L'Allegro* and *Il Penseroso* and *Comus* helped forward the Romantic Revival ; but the chief influence of Milton on the development of English poetry was not this. It was natural enough that those who had been taught from childhood to read and admire *Paradise Lost* should find relief and novelty in the freer and more spontaneous music of these youthful poems. But the truth is that before ever he abetted the escape, he helped to forge the fetters; that Milton, as much as any other single writer, was responsible for the wide and potent sway of the classical convention.

Above all, he may fairly be called the inventor and, by the irony of fate, the promulgator of that "poetic diction" which, in the time of its deformity and decay, Wordsworth sought to destroy. Johnson attributes the invention to Dryden. "There was therefore," he says, "before the time of Dryden no poetical diction, no system of words, at once refined from the grossness of domestick use, and free from the harshness of terms appropriated to particular arts. Words too familiar or too remote defeat the purpose of a poet."

There is no need to quarrel with this account, if we are careful to understand exactly what Johnson means. Dryden, he says in effect, wrote plain, well-bred English ; he eschewed technical terms, shunned the florid licenses of the Elizabethans, and yet, in his more studied verse, never dropped into the town-gallant vein of some of his contemporaries, the slang of Butler or Lestrange. Johnson, it should be remembered, thought the diction of *Lycidas* "harsh," and it is plain enough from many of his utterances that he ranged Milton with the poets who use words and phrases "too remote" from the language of natural intercourse.

He was a devoted adherent of the school of
Dryden and Pope; in the *Lives of the Poets* he
loses no opportunity of expressing his contempt
for blank verse ; he was only too likely to exalt
the influence of his masters on the poets of his
own time, and to ignore the influence of Milton.
Since handbooks of literature are commonly formed
by a process of attrition from such works as
Johnson's *Lives*, his opinions on a point like this
persist in epidemic fashion ; they are detached
from their authority, and repeated so often that
at last they become orthodox.   But no ignoring
of Milton can alter the fact that English verse
went Milton-mad during the earlier half of the
eighteenth century.   Miltonic cadences became a
kind of patter, and the diction that Milton had
invented for the rendering of his colossal imaginations was applied indifferently to all subjects—to
apple-growing, sugar-boiling, the drainage of the
Bedford level, the breeding of negroes, and the
distempers of sheep.   Milton's shadowy grandeur,
his avoidance of plain concrete terms, his manner
of linking adjective with substantive, were all
necessary to him for the describing of his strange
world ; but these habits became a mere vicious
trick of absurd periphrasis and purposeless vagueness when they were carried by his imitators into
the description of common and familiar objects.
A reader making his first acquaintance with

Thomson's *Seasons* might suppose that the poem was written for a wager, to prove that country life may be described, and nothing called by its name. The philosophic pride of the eighteenth century was tickled by the use of general terms in description ; the chosen periphrases are always more comprehensive than the names that they replace. When Thomson, for instance, speaks of " the feathered nations " or of " the glossy kind," it is only by the context that we are saved from supposing him to allude, in the one case to Red Indians, in the other to moles. And these are but two of some dozen devices for escaping from the flat vulgarity of calling birds by that name.

Milton himself, it must be admitted, is not wholly free from blame. The elevation and vagueness of his diction, which were a mere necessity to him in the treatment of large parts of his subject, are yet maintained by him in the description of things comparatively familiar. When Sin is described as " rolling her bestial train " towards the gates of Hell, the diction is faultless ; when the serpent (as yet an innocent reptile in Paradise),

> Insinuating, wove with Gordian twine
> His braided train,

it is impossible to cavil ; but when Raphael, in conversation with Adam, describes the formation of the banks—

> where rivers now
> Stream, and perpetual draw their humid train,

criticism is less at ease. We feel that we are drawing near to the "poetic diction" of the eighteenth century. Eve's tears are called

> precious drops that ready stood
> Each in their crystal sluice,

but the description is saved by the lines that immediately precede, where Milton says the word, and thereby shows that he is not seeking idle periphrasis :—

> But silently a gentle tear let fall
> From either eye, and wiped them with her hair.

His constant preference for words of Latin origin certainly brings Milton near at times to the poetic diction banned by Wordsworth. "Vernal bloom" for "spring flowers," "humid bow" for "rainbow," the description of the brooks rolling—

> With mazy error under pendent shades,

the use of phrases like "nitrous powder" or "smutty grain" for "gunpowder," and "optic glass" or "optic tube" for the telescope or "perspective," are instances of the approximation. A certain number of these circuitous phrases are justified by considerations of dramatic propriety. When Raphael describes the artillery used in Heaven, he speaks of cannon balls as "iron globes" and "balls of missive ruin," and calls the linstock the "incentive reed pernicious," thereby perhaps drawing attention to the strange character of the new invention. No such reason can be invoked for his justification when he tells how the sun receives from earth

> his alimental recompense
> In humid exhalations ;

still less when, speaking of food, with which he confesses himself to be familiar, he calls it "corporal nutriment."

But the chief sinner is Adam. If the evil passions of the rebel Angels invented the pun, it was the pomposity of our father Adam that first brought "poetic diction" into vogue. When the curse has fallen in Eden he makes a long speech for the comfort of Eve, in the course of which he alludes to "the graceful locks of these fair spreading trees," speaks of the sun as "this diurnal star " and, studying protection against the newly experienced cold, advises—

> how we his gathered beams
> Reflected may with matter sere foment,
> Or by collision of two bodies grind
> The air attrite to fire ;

—for all the world as if he were a man of science lecturing to some Philosophic Institute on the customs of savages.

If, then, the term "poetic diction " is to be

used as Wordsworth used it, Johnson's account of its origin must be amended. There was little or no poetic diction, of the kind condemned by Wordsworth, before the time of Milton. In the Elizabethan age all diction was free to poetry, and was freely used. Drawing on his accumulated stores of literary reminiscence, and using them for his own special purpose, Milton invented "poetic diction," and bore a main part in the founding of the English school of poetry which is called "Classical." His diction is called "poetic," because it was absolutely fitted to his purpose, which could have been conceived only by the loftiest poetic genius. His style was admired, misunderstood, and imitated for a century. The diction of his imitators is called "poetic," because, for the most part, they believed that dull nonsense and trading platitudes could be made into poetry by a borrowed system of diction.

Even the best poets of the age are not freer than the rest from the baneful Miltonic infection. Coleridge found the source of "our pseudo-poetic diction" in Pope's *Homer*. But Pope was from boyhood a sedulous student of Milton, and a frequent borrower. The mock-heroics of the *Dunciad* are stilted on Miltonic phrases; and in the translation of Homer, above all, reminiscences of Milton abound. In most of them Milton's phraseology is weakened and misapplied. Two instances among many may serve. When Vulcan, in the First Iliad, warns Juno against rousing the anger of Jove, he adds :—

> Once in your cause I felt his matchless might,
> Hurled headlong downward from th' ethereal height.

The word "flaming" in Milton's splendid line did not suit Pope's purpose—so it disappears, and with it half the glory of the original. In place of it, to eke out the syllables, he inserts the idle, if not foolish, substitute "downward." This is the art of sinking in poetry. Again, Ulysses, narrating his adventures, in the Ninth Odyssey, remarks :—

> In vain Calypso long constrained my stay,
> With sweet, reluctant, amorous delay.

The whole line, so beautiful when it describes the modesty of Eve, in its new context becomes stark nonsense. It is Ulysses, not Calypso, whose delay should be called "reluctant." The misuse of Milton's line makes the situation comic.

James Thomson (to take another example) with a genuine thin vein of originality, too often conceals it under Miltonic lendings. The trail of *Paradise Lost* runs all through *The Seasons*. In such a description as this of the Moon in Autumn there is a cluster of reminiscences :—

> Meanwhile the Moon
> Full-orbed and breaking through the scattered clouds,

Shows her broad visage in the crimsoned east.
Turned to the Sun direct, her spotted disk,
Where mountains rise, umbrageous dales descend,
And caverns deep, as optic tube descries,
A smaller Earth, gives all his blaze again,
Void of its flame, and sheds a softer day.

Thomson could not resist the attractions of Milton's stately Latin vocabulary.   Where Milton describes how, in Paradise—

the flowery lap
Of some irriguous valley spread her store ;

Thomson follows with—

See where the winding vale its lavish stores
Irriguous spreads.

Where Milton describes how Satan, wounded by Michael—

writhed him to and fro convolved,

Thomson follows with a description of the Spring meadows, where

the sportive lambs
This way and that convolved, in friskful glee
Their frolics play.

The lambs emulating Satan are a kind of epitome and emblem of those descriptive poets of the eighteenth century who took Milton for their model.

But perhaps the best example of all is Gray, whose work is full of Miltonic reminiscence.   He frequently borrows ; and, like Pope, almost always spoils in the borrowing. Thus what Milton writes of the nightingale—

> She all night long her amorous descant sung,—

is echoed by Gray in the *Sonnet on the Death of Richard West*:—

> The birds in vain their amorous descant join.

Now a "descant" is a variation imposed upon a plain-song. The word exactly describes the song of the nightingale ; but the addition of the verb "join" robs it of all meaning. Again, the passage in the Second Book of *Paradise Lost* where Moloch describes the pains of Hell—

> when the scourge
> Inexorably, and the torturing hour
> Calls us to penance,—

lingered in Gray's memory when he addressed Adversity—

> Whose iron scourge and torturing hour
> The bad affright, afflict the best.

The "torturing hour" in Gray's lines becomes one of the chance possessions of Adversity, suspended from her belt with the rest of her trinkets. Observe how the word "hour" has been emptied of its meaning. It affrights one class of persons, and afflicts another, which anything that is "torturing" might easily do. In Milton the most awful property of Time is indicated; the hour "calls—inexorably." Here, then, in two cases, is plagiarism, which may be defined as unblest theft—the theft of what you do not want, and cannot use.

In these and many other passages of eighteenth-century verse it may be seen how literary reminiscence sometimes strangles poetry; and how a great man suffers at the hands of his disciples and admirers. The thing has happened so often that it ceases to cause surprise; were not Lydgate and Occleve pupils (save the mark!) of Chaucer? And yet it remains a paradox that Milton's, of all styles in the world, unapproachable in its loftiness, invented by a temper of the most burning zeal and the profoundest gravity for the treatment of a subject wildly intractable by ordinary methods, should have been chosen by a generation of philosophical organ-grinders as the fittest pattern for their professional melodies; and that a system of diction employed by a blind man for the description of an imaginary world should have been borrowed by landscape-gardeners and travelling pedlars for the setting forth of their works and their wares.

EPILOGUE

In the meantime, while Dryden and Milton both had their schools, most of our seventeenth-century poetry fell into an almost complete oblivion. Dryden's satiric, and Milton's epic strains engrossed attention, and shaped the verses of an age. But the seventeenth century was extraordinarily wealthy in poetic kinds quite distinct from these : in metaphysic, and mysticism, in devotional ecstasy, and love-lyric, and romance. The English genius in poetry is essentially metaphysical and romantic. Milton was neither. He could not have excelled in any of these kinds ; nor have come near to Suckling, or Crashaw, or Vaughan, or Herrick, or Marvell, in their proper realms. It is a permissible indulgence, therefore, in taking leave of Milton, to turn from the *Paradise Lost* for a moment, and, escaping from the solid materialism of the heroic and epic strain, to find passion once more among the Court lyrists, and spiritual insight among the retired mystics, to find Religion and Love, and the humility that has access to both.

A profound humility, impossible to Milton, inspired Vaughan when he wrote such a verse as
this :—

> There is in God, some say,
> A deep but dazzling darkness ; as men here
> Say it is late and dusky, because they
> See not all clear.
> O for that night ! where I in him
> Might live invisible and dim !

There is a natural vision, and there is a spiritual
vision ; the spiritual belongs to Vaughan, not to
Milton. If Milton persuades us to a willing
suspension of disbelief for the moment, Vaughan
thrills us with a sense of vivid reality. His *Ascen-
sion Day* is a thing seen, as if it were a memory of
yesterday :—

> The day-star smiles, and light, with thee deceast,
> Now shines in all the chambers of the East.
> What stirs, what posting intercourse and mirth
> Of Saints and Angels glorifie the earth !
> What sighs, what whispers, busie stops and stays ;
> Private and holy talk fill all the ways !
> They pass as at the last great day, and run
> In their white robes to seek the risen Sun ;
> I see them, hear them, mark their haste, and move
> Amongst them, with them, wing'd with faith and love.

To the intensity of his aspiration and hushed
expectance the world seems only a turbulent
passing pageant, or a hard wayfaring, suffered in
a dream :—

Who stays
Here long must passe
O'er dark hills, swift streames, and steep ways
As smooth as glasse.

Or a brief sickness :—

So for this night I linger here,
And, full of tossings to and fro,
Expect still when thou wilt appear,
That I may get me up and go.

His eyes are fixed on the shining lights that beckon
him; the world is full of voices, but its sights and
sounds appeal to him in vain; the beauties that
surround him are things of naught—

Glorious deceptions, gilded mists,
False joyes, phantastick flights.

In the distance before him there shines

An air of glory
Whose light doth trample on my days ;
My days, which are at best but dull and hoary,
Meer glimmering and decays ;

and he lifts up his voice in passionate desire for
the ultimate deliverance :—

Ah ! what time will it come ?   When shall that crie
The Bridegroome's comming ! fill the sky ?
Shall it in the evening run,
When our words and works are done ?
Or will thy all-surprising light
Break at midnight ?

He broods over it till nothing else is present to
him in the night-watches:—

> I saw Eternity the other night
> Like a great ring of calm and endless light.

The history of the struggles and corruption of
mankind may close at any moment, in the twink-
ling of an eye, at a signal given:—

> All's in deep sleep and night; thick darkness lyes
> And hatcheth o'er thy people—
> But hark! what trumpet's that, what angel cries
> *Arise! Thrust in thy sickle!*

Here is a religious poet indeed, a visionary, a
mystic, and a Christian; none of which names can
be truly applied to Milton. And if we wish to
find Love enjoying his just supremacy in poetry,
we cannot do better than seek him among the
lyrists of the Court of Charles II. Milton, self-
sufficient and censorious, denies the name of love
to these songs of the sons of Belial. Love, he
says, reigns and revels in Eden, not

> in court amours,
> Mixed dance, or wanton mask, or midnight ball,
> Or serenate, which the starved lover sings
> To his proud fair, best quitted with disdain.

Yet for the quick and fresh spirit of love in
the poetry of that time we must go to the sons
of Belial. There is a pathetic passage in one of
Milton's divorce pamphlets, where, speaking of

the unhappy choices in marriage to which "soberest and best governed men " are liable, he remarks :— " It is not strange though many, who have spent their youth chastely, are in some things not so quick-sighted while they haste too eagerly to light the nuptial torch ; nor is it therefore that for a modest error a man should forfeit so great a happiness, and no charitable means to release him, since they who have lived most loosely, by reason of their bold accustoming, prove most successful in their matches, because their wild affections, unsettling at will, have been as so many divorces to teach them experience."

The wild affections, unsettling at will, wrote better love-songs than the steadfast principles of the sober and well-governed. Roystering libertines like Sir Charles Sedley were more edifying lovers than the austere husbands of Mary Powell and of Eve. Milton would have despised and detested the pleasure-seeking philosophy of Sedley :—

> Let us then ply those joys we have,
> 'Tis vain to think beyond the grave ;
> Out of our reach the Gods have laid
>   Of Time to come th' event,
> And laugh to see the Fools afraid
>   Of what the Knaves invent.

But the self-abandonment and the passion of two or three of Sedley's songs are out of Milton's reach :—

Not *Celia* that I juster am,
　Or better than the rest,
For I would change each hour like them,
　Were not my heart at rest.

But I am ty'd to very thee
　By every thought I have,
Thy face I only care to see,
　Thy heart I only crave.

All that in woman is ador'd
　In thy dear self I find,
For the whole sex can but afford
　The handsome and the kind.

Why should I then seek further store,
　And still make love anew ;
When change itself can give no more,
　'Tis easie to be true.

It is like a cup of cold water after the didactic endearments of Adam, and his repeated apostrophe :

Daughter of God and Man, immortal Eve—
For such thou art, from sin and blame entire.

Then there was John Wilmot, Earl of Rochester. He was drunk for five years on end,—so his biographer, who had it from his own lips, alleges —and he died at the age of thirty-two. Like Sedley, he professes no virtues, and holds no far-reaching views. But what a delicate turn of personal affection he gives to the expression of his careless creed :—

The time that is to come is not,
How can it then be mine ?
The present moment's all my lot,
And that, as fast as it is got,
Phyllis, is only thine.

Then talk not of inconstancy,
False hearts, and broken vows !
If I by miracle can be
This live-long minute true to thee,
'Tis all that Heaven allows.

Rochester's best love-poetry reaches the topmost pinnacle of achievement in that kind. None has ever been written more movingly beautiful than this :—

When, wearied with a world of woe,
To thy safe bosom I retire,
Where love and peace and truth does flow,
May I contented there expire !

Lest, once more wandering from that heaven,
I fall on some base heart unblest—
Faithless to thee, false, unforgiven—
And lose my everlasting rest !

Or than that other piece (too beautiful and too intense to be cited as a sudden illustration of a thesis) beginning—

Why dost thou shade thy lovely face ? O why
Does that eclipsing hand of thine deny
The sunshine of the Sun's enlivening eye ?

The wind bloweth where it listetn ; the wandering fire of song touches the hearts and lips of whom it will. Milton built an altar in the name of the Lord, and he made a great trench about the altar, and he put the wood in order, and loaded the altar with rich exotic offerings, cassia and nard, odorous gums and balm, and fruit burnished with golden rind. But the fire from Heaven descended on the hastily piled altars of the sons of Belial, and left Milton's gorgeous altar cold.

His fame is now old-established and settled, so there is no place left for the eloquence of the memorialist, or the studied praises of the pleader. I have tried to understand Milton; and have already praised him as well as I know how, with no stinted admiration, I trust, and certainly with no merely superstitious reverence. If I must round my discourse by repeating something that I have already said or suggested, it shall be this—that as he stands far aloof from his contemporaries, so in the succession of great figures that mark for us the centuries of our literature he is seen once more singular and a stranger. We bred Shakespeare in our Midlands; he was nourished from the soil that still grows our daily bread. But Milton was an alien conqueror. The crowd of native-born Puritans, who sometimes (not without many searchings of heart and sharp misgivings) attempt to claim him for their leader, have no title in him. It is a proof of his dominating power, and no credit to their intelligence, that they accept him as their representative. His influence on the destinies and history of our literature might be compared to the achievement of Napoleon while he was winning the victories that changed the map of Europe. He could not change the character of a people, nor perpetuate his dynasty. But nothing is as it would have been without him. Our literature is as hospitable as the Hindoo pantheon ; the great revolutionary has won a place even in our creed. And the writer has this advantage, at least, over the conqueror and legislator, that he has bequeathed to us not maps, nor laws, but poems, whose beauty, like the World's unwithered countenance, is bright as at the day of their creation.

INDEX

[For the following Index I am indebted to the kindness of three of my pupils, Miss F. Marston, Miss E. L. Morice, and Miss D. E. Yates.]

THE END

Printed by R. & R. CLARK, LIMITED, *Edinburgh*

For EU product safety concerns, contact us at Calle de José Abascal, 56–1°,
28003 Madrid, Spain or eugpsr@cambridge.org.

www.ingramcontent.com/pod-product-compliance
Ingram Content Group UK Ltd.
Pitfield, Milton Keynes, MK11 3LW, UK
UKHW010345140625
459647UK00010B/846